JAPAN'S ULTIMATE MARTIAL ART

Jujitsu Before 1882
The Classical Japanese Art
of Self-Defense

DARRELL MAX CRAIG

TUTTLE PUBLISHING
Boston • Rutland, Vermont • Tokyo

First published in 1995 by Tuttle Publishing, an imprint of Periplus Editions (HK) Ltd., with editorial offices at 153 Milk Street, Boston, Massachusetts, 02109.

Library of Congress Cataloging-in-Publication Data

Craig, Darrell.
        Japan's ultimate martial art : jujitsu before 1882 / by Darrell
Max Craig.
        p. cm.
      ISBN 0-8048-3027-4
     I. Jiu-jitsu—Japan—History.   I. Title.
GV1114.C73   1995
796.8' 15' 0952—dc20   95-8843
                   CIP

Distributed by:

North America, Latin America & Europe
Tuttle Publishing
Distribution Center
Airport Industrial Park
364 Innovation Drive
North Clarendon, VT 05759-9436
Tel: 802-773-8930
Fax: 802-773-6993
email: info@tuttlepublishing.com

Japan & Korea
Tuttle Publishing
Yaekari Bldg., 3F
5-4-12 Osaki, Shinagawa-ku
Tokyo 141 0032
Tel: 81-35-437-0171
Fax: 81-35-437-0755
email: tuttle-sales@gol.com

Asia Pacific
Berkeley Books Pte Ltd
130 Joo Seng Road
#06-01/03 Olivine Building
Singapore 368357
Tel: 65-6-280-1330
Fax: 65-6-280-6290
email: inquiries@periplus.com.sg

All photographs (except where credit is given) are by the author.

06 05 04 03   10 9 8 7 6 5 4
Printed in Singapore

This book is dedicated to all those teachers who carry the flickering lantern of light so that others may follow, and to those students who stumble and fall along the path of budo, unable to proceed by themselves.

I would also like to dedicate this work to the one student whose constant nagging caused me to finish it and to Mrs. Mary Schulz.

CONTENTS

PREFACE

I WAS ONCE asked why I wanted to subtitle this book *Jujitsu Before 1882*. At the time, I was unable to come up with an exact answer. All I knew was that the title "felt" appropriate because—as everyone knows—it was in 1882 that judo gained ascendancy and jujitsu began its decline. I now know the answer: today, judo is a sport, with highly detailed rules and regulations. Jujitsu, however, has never been a sport. It has never had any rules, any barred techniques, or any concept of fair play; its only point has been to maim or kill your opponent. It is true that martial arts work best when someone is attacking you; nevertheless, in many jujitsu techniques the technician becomes the aggressor and gives no quarter to his prey.

This book is about jujitsu in all its traditional deadly nature, and about how it was originally taught and applied. Beginning in 1882, some of the techniques demonstrated in this book ceased being taught as widely and frequently as they once were. They have, in a sense, become relics of past glories, anachronisms in today's world. Many of the wonderful old senseis who mastered these techniques and passed them on to future generations are no longer with us. So that their knowledge and teachings will not be lost forever, I am particularly proud to include them in this book.

I suspect that the reader's motivation to purchase this book is similar to that which has recently rekindled an interest in Japan in learning traditional jujitsu methods. Throughout the judo world there are many who realize that modern judo has failed. Many have come to see judo not as its founder, Dr. Jigaro Kano, saw his art in 1882 but as some type of wrestling contest. The true art of what is left of judo lies hidden within its traditional kata. Even that has changed from decade to decade. This book is not about judo per se but about its predecessor, known originally as *yawara* and today as *jujitsu,* or *taiho jitsu.*

It was not until about 1930 that judo actually became fully separated from jujitsu. Until then judo was still referred to as *Kano Jiu Jitsu* ("Jiudo"). As late as 1938 a book published by S. J. Jorgensen referred to Kano Jiu Jitsu as the official jujitsu of the Japanese government. By that time, traditional jujitsu had fallen considerably from the high public stature it previously enjoyed. It was still taught, but mostly by and to ruffians and gamblers: a more refined art, called *aikijitsu,* was now being taught to the upper class.

In some instances it is hard to distinguish between the two arts. The difference lies more in how a technique is taught than in the technique itself. Nevertheless, judo was designed from jujitsu, and aikido was refined through aikijitsu. My first real exposure occurred in 1973, when I was in Japan studying kendo with Sensei Setsuji Kobayashi of the Imperial Palace Police. Through our conversations, I found out that Sensei Ichiro Hata had studied jujitsu, or, as the Japanese now called it, taiho jitsu. Sensei Hata was a government official with a deep and varied experience in Japanese martial arts.

I must admit that the names confused me at first. My first thoughts were that they were two different martial arts. As time passed and I was taken from police gym to police gym to study or observe, I realized that judo or kendo was taught to every policeman, while taiho jitsu was taught only to an elite officer group analogous to what we would call a SWAT (Special Weapons and Tactics) team, men in their middle or late twenties. Their workouts were Monday through Saturday for one hour, and they were the most excruciating I have ever witnessed. I was so impressed by what I saw that, when I returned to the United States, I wrote Sensei Hata a letter inviting him to come to Houston.

About one year later, Sensei Hata arrived for a three-week stay, and I began my study of jujitsu. Since that introduction, I have gone to Japan several times to study with Sensei Hata, and he has returned here several times. The experience has, for me, been invaluable.

The techniques demonstrated in the following chapters are of the Kaisho Goshin Budo Taiho Jitsu Ryu (Kaisho—Tokyo Police; Goshin—self-defense; Budo—martial way; Taiho Jitsu—body techniques). I have deliberately used Japanese terms throughout this book. This may, at times, be frustrating to the reader, but as the international art of ballet uses French terminology, the international art of jujitsu currently relies upon Japanese. To assist the reader, however, I have supplied a glossary of commonly used Japanese terms.

Similarly, because this book concerns itself with classical methods of jujitsu, the illustrations depict classical Japanese attire. Thus, the attacker (*uke*) is always depicted wearing the traditional loincloth (*the heko*), and the defender (*tori*) is always shown wearing the traditional uniform top (*uwagi*) and divided pantlike skirt (*hakama*). I hope these drawings will get the readers in the mood of the times and increase enjoyment of this book. Rest assured: even though the attire may look a little strange, the techniques demonstrated work just as well on today's mean streets as they did centuries ago in the Japanese countryside.

History is made by human activity. Unless history can be observed from the perspective of the personalities who make it, it cannot be fully understood or precisely recorded. The Japanese jujitsu man has played an extremely important role in the history of the Japanese nation, but his role has yet to be fully probed in contemporary writings. In this small attempt to discover more about jujitsu, we pay tribute to the countless and often nameless thousands of persons of the past and the present who have made the art of jujitsu possible.

My special thanks go to three wonderful people of whom I have had the extreme pleasure of being not only teacher but, more importantly, friend. First, Mary Schulz produced the hundreds of drawings found in this book from photographs, penciled stick figures, and sometimes my not-so-accurate memory. Second, Claudia Smith dedicated countless hours to the typing of this manuscript and provided technical advice, sometimes serving as a model reader of the text to clarify the directions. Last, but not least, Gary Grossman expended endless effort in editing, correcting spelling, and sometimes making sense out of something Claudia and I wrote that did not make sense even after we read it.

Additionally, I'd like to thank—though they have already passed through this thing we call life—Master Harutane Chiba of the Hokushin Ito Ryu and Master Ichiro Hata. Without their vast knowledge of the past and their incredible understanding of how to make a technique work in the present, this book would have remained a drawer full of random notes and drawings. Their spirit will live on through these pages.

Without doubt, I have failed to include a photograph of someone who contributed to my martial arts training. For this I apologize. In considering the hundreds of photographs taken throughout the years, I tried to narrow them down to people whom I had practiced with in Japan or those senseis who had given clinics at my dojo. Additionally, if there is a misspelling of a Japanese name, I take full responsibility. Please accept my shortcomings.

I am indebted to all of these sympathetic colleagues, for without their considerable aid, this book would never have been completed.

This book is not meant to be an answer to all questions; it is meant only as a guide to self-improvement. Keep this in mind:

> *There are two people who never have enough time*
> *—The very old and the very young.*

—Author unknown

Darrell Max Craig
Houston, Texas
March 1993

> **"**Metal is tested by fire; man is tested by what he says.**"**
>
> —Master T. Nobushige
> (1525–1561 A.D.)

CHAPTER ONE
Introduction

IT IS SAID that "*ju*" is the heart that may be instructed only by another heart. For that reason, until relatively recently jujitsu techniques were not even written down, much less published. Jujitsu has definitely been a living tradition, one handed down for centuries from teacher to student.

After much personal deliberation and encouragement—bordering on outright nagging—from my students, I concluded that a book on the subject might be a helpful study aid. Accordingly, this book represents what I have learned through my years of practice and conversations with the top taiho jitsu (jujitsu) instructors from Japanese police departments. It reflects the classical art of jujitsu—that is, the traditional techniques of this great art as they have been for centuries—taught in the old Japanese *ryus*.

The student, whether *mudansha* (unranked) or *yudansha* (ranked), who is studying with a qualified teacher hopefully will find this book a source of assistance and enlightenment, but a person who tries to learn techniques using only this book will be confused and discontented. To properly learn any martial art, one must train under a qualified teacher. At best, a book can serve only as a guide. Moreover, many techniques involved in the martial arts can be used to inflict serious injury or death. For example, various judo chokes can cause death or brain damage, and a karate strike or kick can easily be fatal. Jujitsu techniques that utilize nerve and arterial pressure points can be not only excruciatingly painful but also deadly. It therefore is of utmost importance to take the study of a martial art seriously and to train under a qualified teacher who can demonstrate the proper execution of the art's techniques.

The use of a martial art as a method of self-defense is practical, albeit legally touchy. Someone with a weapon has a tremendous advantage over someone without one, especially if he is trained to use that weapon, but jujitsu can be a defense in such a situation. A confrontation between a martial artist and an armed, but untrained, assailant could easily have fatal results for the assailant. The law decides whether a killing is murder or justifiable homicide. If an artist who killed someone admitted to feeling no threat to his life, he might well be found guilty of murder. This scenario may seem improbable, but in your training you must consider how far you are prepared to go in the use of your skills. To give or take a life is not an easy decision. A person who has mastered jujitsu and, more importantly, mastered himself, will always choose to spare life wherever possible.

Since, historically, the method of teaching jujitsu has been more a visual process than a verbal one, I emphasize again the importance of a qualified teacher. But it is my hope that, by studying this book and paying particular attention to its illustrations, the student will learn how to think and react in jujitsu rather than becoming accustomed to being told what to do.

A BRIEF HISTORY OF THE ART

The word *jujitsu* has been known to the western world for centuries. A contemporary dictionary defines *ju-jitsu* (or *ju-jutsu*) as "the Japanese art of defending oneself by grasping or striking an opponent so that his own strength and weight are used against him."[1] The Guinness Book of World Records describes Judo thus: "Origin: Judo is a modern combat sport which developed out of an amalgam of several old Japanese fighting arts, the most popular of which was ju-jitsu, which is thought to be of pre-Christian Chinese origin."[2] One of the better definitions of *jujitsu* was given to me by Sensei Takahiko Ohtsuka. "The term *ju jitsu*" he said, "literally means, technique or art (that is, *jitsu*) of suppleness, flexibility, pliancy, or gentleness (that is, all renditions of the ideogram *ju*)." All these terms, however, represent a single principle, a general way of applying a technique of using the human body as a weapon in unarmed combat. *Jujitsu* literally translates into *ju*, meaning "flexibility or gentleness," and *jitsu*, meaning "art or technique." Judo, a sport more commonly known today, literally translates into *ju* meaning "gentle" and *do* meaning "way." Basically, jujitsu, or techniques of combat, has been converted into judo, or techniques of sport.

In February 1882 at a Buddhist temple called Yeishoji, in a small room of only twelve tatame mats (18 feet by 12 feet) and with only a few dedicated onlookers, birth was given to what we now know as judo. A few years later, on June 10, 1886, in a large, well-lit one-hundred-tatame room at Tokyo Police Headquarters, a contest took place between the new and the old. Jujitsu was represented by the head instructor at the Japanese Police Department. Judo was represented by a student of Dr. Kano; the student was also an aiki-jutsu master. The jujitsu master was beaten and died. From that day forward, judo was the only hand-to-hand self-defense art the upper class would respect and accept. The lower class, trying to copy the upper, followed suit. As a consequence, jujitsu was left to decay as a relic of the past. The decline of jujitsu—this fine and noble art developed by the elite samurai class during Japan's feudal days—symbolized the ending of the feudal system and the beginning of a new era.

The newly formed judo did not have all of the traditional techniques—such as hojo jutsu, yawara jutsu, and jo jutsu—and Sensei Kano had deleted, except in kata, almost all of the hand and foot strikes that were so common to the old jujitsu ryus. However, the Japanese police departments needed these techniques, so, they reorganized their training program, taking techniques that most satisfied their needs. They renamed this art "taiho jitsu," which remains designated for use solely in the Japanese police and national defense forces. Therefore, if you should mention to a Japanese that you study taiho jitsu, his first comment understandably would be, "Oh, you're a policeman." Thus, jujitsu went and taiho jitsu was born.

Yet one may still reasonably inquire: what is jujitsu? Where did it come from, and why don't we hear about it anymore? The word itself has many meanings, from fighting empty-handed to fighting using swords and spears. The one I will exemplify in this book will be the empty-hand jujitsu. Where did it come from? I don't think anyone really knows. Some guidance may be found in the record of Japanese literature called the *Kojiki*, or the Ancient Matters Record. According to Senta Yamada, "The Kojiki describes negotiations between a race of divine origin and a common race over the ownership of land. A member of the common race, Takeminakata-Nu-Kami, dissatisfied over the result of the parle, challenged the representative of the divine race, Takemekazuchi-Nu-Kami, to settle the matter by wrestling."[3] When the challenger lost the contest, the divine race took the land, thus bringing unity to the nation. Some believe that this was the inception of sumo wrestling.

In 22 B.C. another such wrestling match took place between Taima-Nu-Kichaja and Nomi-Nu-Sukune. The outcome was that Nomi-Nu-Sukune threw his opponent to the ground and kicked him to death. This contest supposedly was the inception of what we now call jujitsu. It wasn't, however, until around 1100 A.D. that a very famous samurai named Shinra Suburo Yoshimitsu devised an art from this wrestling type of jujitsu and called it *Daitoryu-Aiki-Ju-Jutsu*.

Daitoryu-Aiki-Ju-Jutsu was different from anything Japan had seen. Before, jujitsu was merely a wild and wooly sport for the amusement of others. Yoshimitsu had taken this so-called sport and devised a system of unarmed self-defense. It proved so successful in combat that, for centuries, it was kept secret and taught only to the Minamoto family, of which Yoshimitsu was a general.

From Yoshimitsu's efforts and success came an assortment of *ryus*, or styles, of jujitsu:

> *Kito-ryu-Ju-Jutsu*—Empty-Hand Arts
> *Jo-Jutsu*—Four-Foot-Stick Art
> *Bo-Jutsu*—Six-Foot-Stick Art
> *Yagyu-ryu-Ju-Jutsu*—Empty-Hand Arts
> *Kumi-uchi-Ju-Jutsu*—Armor Grappling
> *Uchi-ne-Ju-Jutsu*—Throwing Arrows by Hand
> *Tetsubo-Jutsu*—Six-Foot-Iron-Bar Art
> *Aioi-ryu-Jutsu*—Empty-Hand Arts
> *Gekigan-Jutsu*—Ball-and-Chain Arts
> *Kusarigama-Jutsu*—Sickle-and-Chain Arts
> *So-Jutsu*—Spear Arts
> *Hozoin-ryu-Jutsu*—Empty-Hand Arts
> *Genkotsu*—Vital-Points Empty-Hand Arts
> *Daito-ryu-Jutsu*—Empty-Hand Arts

We could go on and on, for there is said to be forty-four jutsus, some with weapons, some without. I do not think, however, that there is a complete list of all the jutsus in existence.

During the Muromachi period (1333–1573), each part of Japan had its own type of jujitsu. Great and small battles took place all over Japan; every lord fought someone for something. Sometimes I think they fought just to keep in practice. Nevertheless, it was a great time to test new fighting techniques. Where else could an upstanding jujitsu master experiment to the death?

Throughout the Muromachi period, jujitsu was most commonly used against armor-clad warriors. But toward the turn of the seventeenth century, as the masterless warriors (*ronin*) appeared in the countryside, jujitsu took a new slant. The large wars were over, and a new type of peace settled over the land. The ruling lords encouraged the establishment of private schools of unarmed and armed arts. The mold was thus made and, by the eighteenth century, jujitsu as an empty-handed way of self-defense seems to have become a general, well-established art. So from the eighteenth century on, as Ratti and Westbrook describe it,

> *[a] growing number of schools began to specialize in methods of unarmed bujutsu. Considering the basic instrumental and functional possibilities of the human body in unarmed combat (upon which the instruction programs of all these schools were based), it might seem odd that there should have been so many different schools scattered throughout the length and breadth of Japan.*[4]

I think it is safe to surmise that all of these schools were offspring of a home school of some type. Each school (*dojo*) had its own particular well-guarded secrets. As E. J. Harrison put it, "The Kito ryu were famous for their techniques of projection; others such as the Takenouchi ryu were noted for the perfection of their techniques of immobilization; still others, such as the Tenjin-Shinyo ryu, were famed for the power of their techniques of percussion."[5]

During this transition period, two types of training developed. In the first, *Ju-Jutsu*, most of the techniques taught were designed to attack the opponent and to defend against his attacks. They generally involved armor-clad samurai and were developed mostly from the combat experience of the bushi, or samurai. It is my opinion that these techniques were still an unpolished gem—highly workable and effective for the purpose for which they were originally designed—but Japan was changing: there were fewer wars, and heavy armor was becoming a relic of the past.

The second type of jutsu, *Aiki-Jutsu*, had broken away from the old body. According to E. J. Harrison, "This school specialized in the teaching of so-called *Aiki-Jutsu*, which was kept secret and disclosed to only a few disciples—for the most part, nobles of ancient lineage. This art had originated from Ken-Jutsu, or swordsmanship, and little by little it had become an art of combat superior to Ju-Jutsu."[6]

Like the *ju* in jujitsu, *aiki* also indicates a way of applying almost any technique successfully against an opponent. I believe that what distinguished aiki-jutsu from jujitsu was the mental training and the use of a person's inner energy, called *ki*. Aiki-jutsu was also taught as a total defense against the attacking opponent. I find that many jujitsu techniques work only if you are stronger than your opponent. Aiki-jutsu, on the other hand, was designed to use the other man's strength with your knowledge of how he is employing it. The theory behind aiki-jutsu is if he does not attack, let him go. The theory of jujitsu is if he does not attack, attack him first.

Jujitsu has always had contests to see who is the superior. Aiki-jutsu never had to be proven except defensively, and then only when necessary. In 1910 a master of the art named Dr. Sogaku Takeda took a young man of twenty-eight as his disciple. The young man soon developed his own ideas of aiki-jutsu into an art called *aikido*. This young man was Morihei Uyeshiba, whose aikido prospers in Japan to this very day. Although there are still several aiki-jutsu schools operating, they are slowly fading into the shadows of time, and I feel they will someday be completely lost.

Another style of jitsu that broke away from the main body—long before Professor

Uyeshiba's aikido—was known throughout Japan as Kano's Ju-Jutsu. Master Jigoro Kano was a master of jujitsu in his own right, having studied many styles of jujitsu, including Kito ryu, Tenshin-Shinyo ryu, Takenouchi ryu, and Sosuishitsu ryu. Dr. Kano could see that jujitsu was slowly on the decline, for fewer students were practicing the art. I am sure he realized that this decline was largely owing to the "no techniques barred" attitude of tournaments. Understandably, many young men were unwilling to sacrifice their lives to learn. As Harrison wrote, "In those days contests were extremely rough and frequently cost the participants their lives. Thus, whenever I sallied forth to take part in any of those affairs, I invariably bade farewell to my parents, since I had no assurance that I should ever return alive."[7]

In 1882, therefore, Dr. Kano formed his new style of jujitsu. He barred many of the old techniques so as to ensure the safety of contestants. Not wanting to eliminate the traditions of the old styles, however, he devised a series of katas to enable a person to practice the old jujitsu techniques without actually using them in a contest. Dr. Kano then proceeded to establish contest rules for this new style:[8]

1. *Each contestant shall wear coat and belt.*
2. *A contestant shall be deemed to have been defeated when his two shoulders and hips shall have touched the floor, provided that said contestant shall have reached this position on the floor through having been thrown down.*
3. *A contestant shall be deemed to have been defeated when in such position on the floor, if said combatant cannot free himself from his opponent's arms within two seconds' time.*
4. *A contestant shall be deemed to have been defeated when from any cause or causes he may become unconscious. But it is not permitted to use serious tricks when the wrestling bout is between friends. Such tricks as kicking and the breaking of arms, legs, and neck are barred.*
5. *A combatant shall be deemed to have been defeated when he has been reduced to submission through the employment by his opponent of any hold or trick.*
6. *When a defeated combatant finds himself obliged to acknowledge his submission, he must pat or hit the floor or his antagonist's body, or somewhere, with his hand or foot. This patting with foot or hand is to be regarded as a token of surrender.*
7. *When a defeated combatant pats or hits the floor, or anywhere, in token of submission, the victor must at once let go his hold.*

There were ten rules in all. Dr. Kano's interesting modifications of these rules were designed for the preservation of his new art. Especially interesting are those designed for a contest with someone utilizing an art different from his own:[9]

1. *It is understood and agreed that the Ju-Jutsu man, whether he fights a boxer or contests with a wrestler, shall be allowed to use in his defense any of the tricks that belong to the art of Ju-Jutsu.*
2. *It is further understood and agreed that the Ju-Jutsu man assumes no responsibility for any injury or injuries caused by any act or thing done during the contest, and that the Ju-Jutsu man shall be held free and blameless for any such ill effect or injury that may be received during the contest.*

> *3. Two competent witnesses representing each side, or four in all, shall see to it that these articles of agreement are properly drawn, signed, and witnessed, to the end that neither contestant–or other participant in the match shall have cause for action on any ground or grounds resulting from any injury or injuries, or death, caused during the contest.*

As to my personal opinion of how jujitsu came about, I agree with Sensei G. Koizumi, Kodokan 7th Dan, who stated:

> *As to the origin and native land of Ju Jutsu, there are several opinions, but they are found to be mere assumptions based on narratives relating to the founding of certain schools, or some incidental records or illustrations found in the ancient manuscripts not only in Japan but in China, Persia, Germany, and Egypt. There is no record by which the origins of Ju Jutsu can be definitely established. It would, however, be rational to assume that ever since the creation, with the instinct of self-preservation, man has had to fight for existence, and was inspired to develop an art or skill to implement the body mechanism for this purpose. In such efforts, the development may have taken various courses according to the condition of life or tribal circumstance, but the object and mechanics of the body being common, the results could not have been so very different from each other. No doubt this is the reason for finding records relating to the practice of arts similar to Ju Jutsu in various parts of the world, and also for the lack of records of its origins.*[10]

NO JU IN THE MASTER

As in my last book, *Iai, The Art of Drawing the Sword,* I have tried here to transport myself back into the time period being written about. So let your mind wander back to the sixteenth century of Japan and read the following story about Komto-Okuda.

* * *

Komto-Okuda was said to be the greatest living jujitsu master in Japan. Many students of the art tested their skills against him, but none ever prevailed. Most, in fact, were beaten long before their hands ever reached toward the master. At the time of this story, Komto was a man about fifty years old, with an average build. He kept his head shaved and had an air of humility. His most distinctive feature was his eyes, which generated a mysterious feeling. They seemed to look directly into your mind and to allow him to read your thoughts. A close look into his eyes sent a chill down your back. Yet, deep inside, you felt a warmth of understanding in him.

One day, as the sun was slowly descending behind the mountain and the chill of the evening was crawling upon the little monastery where Komto lived, a young man in his teens appeared at the outer gates. His name was Soto Mamoto. He had come a great distance. A Zen priest was lighting the gate lantern when the young man asked, "Is this the monastery where Master Komto-Okuda resides?" Not stopping his duties, the priest pointed to a small door within the gates. The young man bowed quickly and started toward the door. Just as he was about to let his presence be known, the small door slid open, revealing a man standing there. The young man was momentarily startled and did not know what to say. Then, dropping to his knees, he spoke.

"Oh, please master, you must teach me to be a master of jujitsu like yourself."

The man in the door remained silent for what seemed like an eternity to the young man. Then, as quickly as the door opened, it shut. The young man could not believe that, after giving up everything to seek out the master, the master had shut the door on him. Well, this just would not do; no one—master or not—was going to shut a door in his face, without at least answering the question he had come so far to ask. Jumping to his feet, the young man ran up the two small steps and, knocking on the door, proclaimed in a loud voice, "You in there, who so rudely shut this door. I demand you come back out here and speak to me. I have but one question to ask, and you will answer it before this night is through or my name is not Soto Mamoto."

The door slid open, as if by mysterious powers of its own. And there, out of nowhere, stood Komto-Okuda. As Soto looked into the master's eyes, he felt his knees bend slightly, and he knew it was not for the purpose of bowing. Looking deep into Soto's eyes—almost as if he were looking through him—and not changing his facial expression or raising his voice, Komto said, "I hope your question is worthy of the answer."

As Soto's head started to clear, he found himself on the ground in front of the small closed door. Lying there, slowly moving his head from left to right, he was convinced that he had been hit from behind. But, to his surprise, he was all alone, with nothing but the flickering of the candle disturbing the stillness. He just could not believe it; one minute he was on the step and the next second on the ground. Now more than ever, Soto felt compelled to become a student of this man.

As the dampness of the evening dew crept into Soto's kimono, it suddenly occurred to him to open the door and confront the master. He started to rise, but his head hurt so terribly that the thought quickly vanished.

Slowly taking a kneeling position in front of the steps, Soto waited. "The master has to come through the door sooner or later," Soto surmised, "and when he does he will see how humble I have made myself. Then he will have to accept me as his student."

Minutes turned into hours, and the hours brought the cold mountain night. His eyes began to close, and he fell into a deep slumber. When next he opened them, he felt the warmth of the morning sun on his back. Quickly looking up at the door, he saw that it was still shut. "Good," he thought, "he has not left yet and, when he does, I will be waiting." Morning turned into afternoon and his legs began to ache. His back felt as if trampled by an oxen and his throat was parched. "Why does not the master come out?" he thought. "I do not know if I can stay here much longer."

Suddenly there was an indescribable pain across his back. Again and again he felt a stick come crashing down upon him. As he tried to get to his feet to deflect the blows, he found that his legs would not cooperate, and he tumbled, falling flat on his face. Then the blows changed from his back to his buttocks. He pulled with his arms using all the strength left in his body until he was under the steps and safe from the madman. Looking through the steps at his attacker, he saw Komto-Okuda shoulder a long piece of bamboo and laugh to the heavens. Komto's voice roared with laughter, "Where is this man who demands to ask me but one question? Could that be him I see under my house? He demanded last night, and now he acts like a dog and hides beneath my dwelling." As the words echoed, Komto went up the steps and the door closed. Kneeling under the steps, trying to get the blood to circulate again in his legs, Soto could not help thinking to himself, "This man is stark raving mad. No wonder he's known as the greatest jujitsu master alive: a person would have to be mad to deal with such a man." Just then he heard the door slide open above him, and a torrent of water came pouring down upon him. "There, Demanding One with no manners, let me try and clean your outside while you do something with that you call a brain."

That was enough. Out from under the steps Soto came. "Master" he shouted, "if you are not going to accept me as your student, then at least say so and I will be on my way." "Accept you?" Komto laughed, "Ha! Haa! You who came to me first demanding, then tried to show humility by kneeling all night outside my door, but was without enough humility to stay awake. Want you? No, I do not want you." "So!" Soto broke in, "I will be on my way! Maybe I did start off on the wrong foot, and maybe I deserved the beating, but after all I have been through, don't you think you could at least answer my question?"

Komto put his finger to the side of his nose and looked straight into Soto's face. For the first time Soto began to know fear. With a half-smile on his face but a frown upon his brow, Komto said almost in a whisper, "Tell me, little one, not that it really matters, what is your question?" Komto started down the steps, slowly placing his hands on the bamboo stick. "Come here so we can talk, little one." He was still moving forward toward Soto. Soto felt he was in a dream; he could feel the master getting closer, but he did not seem to see his body moving. Komto reached out with his right hand and grabbed the boy by his hair. "Now Demanding One," Komto exclaimed, holding him so that his face looked straight into the afternoon sun, "tell me what is this most important question?" Soto felt his neck about to break from the pressure of the master's grip and knew he was either about to die or have his question answered.

"What is this question, Demanding One?" Komto said again softly, with eyes ablaze.

"Let go of my hair so I can stand up and I will tell you," Soto replied. As Komto released his grip it seemed to Soto that the hair on his head had grown a foot. Now Soto dropped to his knees at the master's feet and, without looking up, started to explain his question.

"Master, as I have said, my name is Soto Mamoto and I come from Kyushu. My father was a samurai at Kumamoto Castle until he was killed by two ruthless ronin six months ago. It was at this time I started on my journey to find you, master."

Komto broke in, "What was your father's name, little one?"

"Shin No Fuji Mamoto," Soto replied.

"Not Shin No Fuji Mamoto of Higo Prefecture?"

"Yes," Soto replied.

Komto could scarcely believe it. Shin No Fuji and he had grown up together, had fought side-by-side in the castle wars, had gotten drunk together many times, and eventually had fallen in love with the same woman. But he had not heard from his good friend in many years. Quickly, Komto's mind snapped back to the boy. "Tell me, little one, what was your mother's name? And is she not worried about her son so far away at a time she might need him most?" he demanded.

"Master, her name was Shimoke-Kuto, but she died when I was born, and I only know of her from my father's uncle. My father would never let her name be spoken in his presence."

Komto reached down and put his hand under the boy's chin, lifting it so he could study the story on his face. Indeed, Komto thought, this is Shimoke's child. She was the most beautiful woman he had ever known, and through this little one she still lived.

Just then a loud voice from the monastery gate cut short Komto's memories. The voice was so loud that it startled Soto, and he jumped to his feet. Komto reached out and pushed the boy behind him. Two men stood at the gate. Komto placed his hands inside his kimono, turned to face them and spoke, "My name is Komto-Okuda. What do you seek here?"

One of the men replied, "We do not wish you harm, old man. We have come for that one, there," and pointed at the young man.

"And what do you wish of him, may I ask?" questioned Komto.

"That is none of your business," answered the ronin and moved toward Komto.

"But you see it is my business, Smelly One, for the one you seek is my student and therefore I am responsible for all of his actions," Komto retorted.

The ronin laughed smugly, then said, "So, Bold One who is acquainted with the Gods, you are responsible for this little one. Then I suggest that you make yourself ready to meet your responsibilities."

Komto remained silent and let his body relax. He studied the ronin's eyes, never changing his own expression or removing his hands from under his kimono. As the ronin drew his katana, Konto's entire body became only a blur to Soto's eyes. Even more unbelievable to the young man was that the attacking ronin's body now lay lifeless staring into eternity; with the quickness of a mountain cat Komto had broken his neck. Komto quickly turned to face the other ronin, but he had vanished as suddenly as the life which Komto had just taken. Soto's heart pounded like an attack drum and, realizing that the threat was over, he ran to Komto's side. Looking down at the dead ronin and then to the master, Soto began to weep.

"Master, these were the samurai who killed my father! As my father was dying, he told me of you. He said to come here and become your student."

"Not now, little one," Komto interrupted, "we will have plenty of time later to talk about such things. We must take care of first things first. We must care for this lifeless body and pray for his misguided soul. Now go to my room and try to rest while I take care of these matters."

It was late evening when Soto awoke and heard the master come in. He lay there, thinking that never before had he known such a man, such a great warrior. He knew that the answer to his question was within reach.

When Soto awoke the next morning, he could see the master making tea. Quickly going over to Komto, he knelt down and, taking the kettle from the fire, began to pour the master's tea. "If I am going to be your student, master, you must allow me to do my duties. A student does not sleep while his master makes tea."

"It is good you know such things," Komto smiled. As they sipped their tea and warmed their bodies by the fire, Komto broke the silence and said, "Well, little one, I feel it is time we had our talk. You have come all this way to ask a question, but I must warn you that some questions are better never asked, for once you ask and seek the answer, you will be drawn into the trap of life. The answer could lure you away from all things that now seem important. You may start on the endless circle I have traveled, and find only that the end is no end at all. The revenge you hold in your heart for this other man may only bear bitter fruit, that neither you nor anyone else will ever be able to digest. With these things in mind, you may ask your question."

Soto looked reflectively at the master for a minute, put his cup down, and began to speak. "Master, before my father died he made me promise to revenge his death. But in a way, I do not understand. He said I would only be able to set his spirit at rest by finding the answer to the sound of one hand clapping. He said that, unless I truly find this answer, the ronin would surely kill me and my death would be of no purpose. He then told me of you and explained that, if there was anyone on earth who could help me with the problem, it would be you."

Looking into his teacup, Komto could not help but smile to himself, for he knew now without a doubt what he had suspected all along. Shin No Fuji had sent the little one on an endless journey for his own safety. He knew that Soto would never leave the monastery until he had found the answer, and that finding the answer would take many years. By the time Soto knew and understood the answer, he would have forgotten why it was once so important.

Soto cleared his throat and the master looked up. The young man continued, "Master, do you know the answer?"

"Oh yes, I know the answer, little one; but first let me ask you a question. Do you know the sound of two hands clapping?"

"Is it important to know the sound of two hands, master?" Soto replied. Komto poured a little more tea.

"Yes, I am afraid so, little one. Before you get into the water, you must first learn to swim. Remember, if you are going to be my student and search for the answer of one hand, I can only show you the way. I cannot teach you; you must teach yourself. The sound of two hands clapping is one of the most vital elements in the art of jujitsu as well as in zen. Always remember, little one, when the hands are clapped, the sound is heard without a moment's deliberation. If there is any room left even for a breath of air between these two actions, there is interruption. The sound does not wait and think before it issues; one movement follows another without being interrupted by one's conscious mind. Do you understand this, little one?"

"I must confess, master, I do not think I do," Soto replied.

"Well, do not worry now," Komto smiled. "We have plenty of time, and you must start your duties before the morning wastes away."

★ ★ ★

As the young man, Soto, had to begin at the beginning, so do we with proper dojo etiquette and care of the practice uniform, the *hakama* and *uwagi*. But first a few words about training in general and about Japan, in particular.

TRAINING

My sensei once told me:

> 1. A Budo Man in training is in Budo.
> 2. Strength comes from health.
> 3. Speed comes from effort.
> 4. Technique comes from experience.
> 5. Willpower comes from faith.
> 6. Serenity comes from old knowledge.
> 7. Progress comes from new knowledge.

There is a major difference between a trick and a technique. A true technique involves the skillful execution of timing, balance, posture, coordination, and speed and will always work if properly executed. Its development and mastery depend entirely on your personal commitment to training. Jujitsu training requires practicing at the dojo at least twice—preferably three times—a week. But true training requires more than just practicing techniques at the dojo; it requires a change in one's way of life. One must train oneself both physically and mentally. In jujitsu, extreme mental discipline is both a requirement and a result.

One part of mental training is anticipation—that is, expecting a situation and acting upon it. This part of training occurs as much—if not more—outside the dojo as inside. For example, take the scenario of a person walking toward you on the street. Train by looking at his hands. Are they swinging normally at his sides, or is one hand hidden, or are both? If the latter, then something may be amiss and you need to be prepared to act. Train by looking at his belt, his wallet pocket (if he has turned so that you can see it), his wrist with a watch, or the shoulder over which his workout bag is slung; these can offer clues as to whether the person is right- or left-handed, information that can be useful in self-defense. Then look at his eyes, for they are the windows to the mind. If you feel safe with an approaching person, let your concentration go to the next person, but always keep a comfortable and safe personal distance from people. Above all, such observations serve to keep you mentally alert to the people and things around you.

The deadliest part of true jujitsu is never seen by the naked eye. Jujitsu is thus very analogous to an iceberg, whose size you cannot readily determine because its greater part lies below the water line. The same principle of appearance masking inner strength applies to jujitsu techniques. The old masters of Japan intentionally designed the techniques so that their deadly aspects would not be easily discernable and thus fall into their enemies' hands. The techniques were probably also taught this way so that only the most dedicated students would learn their real secrets. Jujitsu also reminds me of the blister gas we were lectured about in the Marines: it has no odor, yet breathing it would cause large internal blisters and death. Jujitsu is similarly deceptive in that it contains rather harmless-looking techniques which carry enormous hidden potential. In the hands of an experienced martial artist, these techniques can easily cripple or kill.

When one trains with a professional teacher in the art, he can easily copy the movements. But merely to copy the movements is only part of the art; some teachers in Japan call this outward motion "rice bowl art." The rice bowl method of training has the advantage of teaching immature students the basics of certain techniques and, at the same time, giving them practice in the basic principles of jujitsu—timing, balance, posture, coordination, and speed. The sensei thus gives this student the lock but not the hidden art—that is, the force, the power, the *key*. This key is given only when the sensei concludes that a student is sufficiently mature to use it properly.

The term *fukushiki-kokyu*, which we will address more fully in Chapter Five, is not a familiar one. Its meaning was not known to me until several years ago when I invited an aikido master of the Yoshinkan style to give a seminar. While he was here, I had an opportunity to inquire as to the term's origin. He felt strongly that it had something to do with what the aikido people refer to as *ki*. The concept of ki, which is most certainly an essential part of all *aikido,* is simply described as "martial force." The words ki and kiai have been treated as technical terms within the classical bujutsu ryus; they are found in the *makimono* (hand scrolls) of the Hokushinkan Chiba Ryu. In connection with the terms *ki* and *kiai*, we cannot omit *okuden* (secret teachings). It is the okuden, not the ki or kiai, that make the teachings truly effective.

The oldest book to discuss ki or kiai is *Budo Hiketsu-Aiki no Jutsu* (*The Secret of Budo*), published in 1899. It states: "The most profound and mysterious art in the world is the art of aiki. This is the secret principle of all the martial arts in Japan. One who masters it can be an unparalleled martial genius." Another book published in 1913, *Jujitsu Kyoju-sho Ryu no Maki* (*Textbook of Jujitsu*), states: "Aiki is an impassive state of mind without a blind side, slackness, evil intention, or fear. There is no difference between aiki and kiai; however, if compared, when expressed dynamically aiki is called ki-ai, and when expressed statically, it is aiki." Still another book published in 1917, called *Goshin-jutsu Ogi* (*The Secret Principles of the Art of Self-Defense*), states that "Ki-kiai or aiki-ho is the technique used to stop the enemy's attack by gaining the initiative over him." *Ki*, or *kiai*, has many meanings. It is translated by some Japanese as "breath"; to others, it means "spirit." Still others think of it as "nervous energy." Perhaps ki is best described as the electricity that flows back and forth throughout your body. It is what gives jujitsu its power and potential deadly effect.

Technique is essential in any martial art, but a practitioner who learns only the technique is not a true martial artist. To become a true artist, the jujitsu practitioner must develop three essential elements: technique *(waza)*, mind and spirit *(shin)*, and, most certainly, activity of our universal subconscious electricity *(ki)*. This can be accomplished only under the watchful eyes of a true master.

Many people involved in Japanese martial arts sooner or later get the urge to train in Japan. I think that is a good idea, so let us discuss the people, the country, and the traditions. It's most important that you understand something about each of these aspects.

According to Japanese mythology, as compiled in the epic *Kojiki*, the islands of Japan were created by the god Izanagi and the goddess Izanami. The legend has the couple perched on top of the "floating bridge of heaven" and stirring the ocean with a holy sword received from Amatsukami, the God of Heaven. When they raised the sword from the waters, ocean salt dripped from the tip of the sword. It fell back to the ocean and accumulated to form the Isle of Onogoro. The two gods then descended to this island, married, and gave birth to island upon island until the archipelago was complete. The storytellers of ancient times passed this myth from generation to generation; undoubtedly they based their tale on how they imagined the Japanese island chain would appear if viewed from high in the heavens.

Japan is made up of more than three thousand islands. The four major ones are Honshu, Shikoku, Kyushu, and Hokkaido. The Japanese people are surrounded on all sides by exquisite natural landscapes. Their daily lives are anchored to the small flatland areas. The Meiji Restoration of 1868 and the forbidding of the samurai to wear their swords forced the industrialization of Japan and increased the importance of the plains. Today the great majority of Japan's population live in the large cities. There you will find the best martial arts schools in the world.

Japan, being composed of a series of islands, has always been somewhat isolated geographically. At various times in its history, however, Japan has also chosen to isolate itself politically. The longest period of isolation, 215 years, ended in 1853 when Admiral Perry appeared with his "black ships" off Uraga, south of Tokyo. Whether the Japanese liked it or not, their country was going to be opened to an influx of western culture, thereby changing the course of Japanese history.

The Japanese had several possible choices in responding to Admiral Perry's ships. They could reject the foreign intrusion outright, ignoring the demands to open Japan for western intercourse, or they could warmly open their arms to western culture. Some chose the former, some the latter, but most chose a course somewhere in between. In general, the Japanese carefully imported western culture, all the while leaving their own culture unaffected. During this period, there was a popular expression, "Wakon yo sai," meaning "western learning, Japanese spirit." In the ten-year span after western culture was first introduced, western culture and technology were widely accepted, but the underlying western thinking was not.

You can do many things to try to understand the Japanese. You can visit their countryside and discover a people at harmony with nature. You can gaze upon a Japanese garden and see how a refined sensitivity can create its own kind of balance. You can get a letter of introduction and stay at a dojo. You can live, train, and learn with the Japanese, or rather relearn the importance of personal relations and group cooperation. You can delve into their religion and philosophy and discover a nation blessedly free of dogma and ideological bias. Or you can simply eat the food and find that not only is it small and beautiful; it is simple.

When you have discovered all these things, there will be at least one more thing you will want to know: Why did the Japanese develop in this unusual way? Did they do so by accident or are all of these cultural threads part of some consistent pattern? Why didn't other people—for instance, the Chinese, who contributed much to Japanese culture—develop in the same way? I have not heard convincing answers. The reason could be quite simple: there is no need for an answer. The Japanese have simply taken the instinctive side of the human personality and refined it to provide the basis of their society.

If you visit a Japanese dojo, you may find it unusual. They have air conditioning only in the winter and heating only in the summer. My first introduction into a dojo was in winter. When my sensei took me to the training hall, everyone was bustling around getting ready for practice. The temperature in the dressing room was reasonably comfortable. After I was dressed, sensei hurried me up the stairs to the practice hall. When I went through the practice hall door, not only did my heart skip a beat, but I thought my feet were going to stick to the wooden floor. The cold inside was like nothing I had expected. The big drum sounded and we all took our places, waiting for the master to appear. When he came in, he spoke in a loud voice. About ten students jumped to their feet and ran in all directions to open all the windows in the hall. The cold winter air went through me like a sword and cut me to the bone. For the first time in my life, I thought that I might have bitten off more than I could chew. Needless to say, the workout was a chilling experience.

Japan has four distinct seasons. Summer is hot and humid, while winter can be unbelievably cold. These extremes are relieved by the seasonal changes, with spring and autumn being exceptionally mild. One of the most remarkable things about Japan's four seasons is that they come and go with clockwork regularity. Though there is not a defined rainy season in Japan, there are varied degrees of precipitation occurring each month of the year. From spring through summer, a long wet season drags on. When the summer heat withdraws its muggy clutches, the typhoon season arrives.

When I go to Japan for training now, I usually try for spring or autumn. Not only are these times the best for training, but the countryside is then beautiful to behold. The few times I have been in Japan during the winter, I trained in Osaka or Tokyo, where blue skies usually prevail. However, crossing over the mountains to the Japanese seaside, you will be greeted by heavy snowfalls. Chilly seasonal winds from Siberia literally inhale ocean water, freezing it into snow which blankets the coast and immediate inland.

As for the Japanese themselves, there is an old saying, "To understand the Japanese, you have to be Japanese." I have been dealing with the Japanese for over thirty years and I find that statement to be generally true. I can say this for sure: as long as you do not try to understand them, you can get along very well. They understand that you are a foreigner in their country and they take great pride in trying to introduce you to their culture. If you go to Japan to train in Budo, you are expected to know how to behave in a dojo. When you speak a "little" Japanese and if you have previously trained under a Japanese sensei, a lot more is expected of you. Usually, if you make too many mistakes, they will not say much, but don't be surprised if you aren't invited back to their dojo. One of the most important things is to just watch and listen to the sensei. Never try to explain to the sensei that what he is teaching you isn't the way you were taught. As long as you remain eager to learn, he will be eager to teach you.

Dojo is a word most martial arts students are familiar with, though many students erroneously associate it with the word *school*, as in high school or college. The dojo, however, is a place where *only* martial arts are taught and, strictly translated, it implies the instruction of only the "true Japanese martial arts" of Ken-Jutsu, Ju-Jutsu, and Kyu-Jutsu. It is more than a gymnasium or club; it is a cherished place of learning and brotherhood.

The Japanese use a broad interpretation of the word. To them, *dojo* is symbolic of the methodical, ideological, philosophical, and, most importantly, the spiritual aspects of the martial arts. Jujitsu involves more than physical techniques; it involves the molding of one's character, the training of one's mind, and—last, but not least—the developing of one's body. The dojo's foundation is based on the idea of virtue. Keep in mind that students of martial arts today are, in effect, the descendants of the samurai of yesteryear. Today's students should work toward the propagation of the spirit of the Zen warrior, a spirit that encompasses more than an expert knowledge of lethal fighting techniques. It represents the attainment of a virtuous way of life where the main theme is the code of Bushido—The Way of the Warrior.

Peter Urban describes the term *dojo* as follows:

> *A traditional dojo is, in a sense, a patriarchy. The sensei (meaning "Honorable Teacher") is the master. The sensei regards his students as his many sons and daughters, seeing them as they can never see themselves. He effects the development of their bodies and their characters. This is the responsibility of his art. The dojo is really the home of the sensei; students come to his home to learn his way of life, the martial arts. All traditional dojos are created by the sensei and maintain the standards of simplicity and beauty found in the original dojos, which always had a shrine built in the highest possible position, symbolizing the dojo's dedication to the virtues and values of its style. All dojos should have time allotted for the practice of meditation, which aids in developing the spiritual teaching and mental training underlying all the martial arts.[11]*

Each dojo is connected with a style (*ryu*) that the master has learned through years of practicing with other ryus. When he develops his own ryu, he usually names it after some particular shrine and technique to distinguish it from other styles, and he is particularly careful to keep its secrets from nonmembers. Even today, in the twentieth century, there are ryus in Japan that have not surfaced completely. The Katori Shinto-Ryu, for example, under its twentieth headmaster, Shuri-No-Suke Yasusada, only recently opened its doors to the western world. To put this fact into historical perspective and give the reader some insight as to its significance, the Katori Shinto-Ryu, originally called Tenshin Shoden Katori Shinto-Ryu, was founded by Iizasa Choisai Lenao between 1387 and 1488. This ryu consists of Iai-Jutsu, Ken-Jutsu, Bo-Jutsu, Nagenata-Jutsu, Ju-Jutsu,

Shuriken-Jutsu, Nin-Jutsu, So-Jutsu, Den-Jutsu, and Chikujo-Jutsu. Even though the ryu has opened its doors to outsiders, it retains its traditional customs. For example, a "candidate for study in the ryu is required to execute the Keppan; to draw and sign in his own blood an oath to abide by the policies of the ryu."[12] The oath and pledge consist of the following:[13]

> 1. *When I become a member of the Tenshin Shoden Katori Shinto-Ryu, which has been handed down by the Great Deity of the Katori Shrine, I therewith affirm my pledge of absolute secrecy about matters of this ryu.*
> 2. *I will not have the impertinence to discuss or demonstrate my martial technique to nonmembers.*
> 3. *I will never engage in any kind of gambling nor frequent disreputable places.*
> 4. *I will not cross swords with any followers of other martial traditions without a certificate of full proficiency in my art.*
> 5. *I now pledge to firmly keep each of the above articles. Should I break any of these articles I will submit to the punishment of the Buddhist deity Marishiten. Herewith, I solemnly swear and affix my blood seal to this oath to the Great Deity.*

As you can see, even with the opening of their doors, they have been careful to see that the style maintains its high standards.

In a traditional dojo, the senior student, on a signal from the master, calls all students to practice by hitting a large drum several times. The students assume the formal sitting position, in accordance with their rank. When the master is satisfied, he walks onto the dojo floor and takes his position of honor in front of the shrine, facing his students. At this time, the senior student calls out in a loud and strong voice, *"Mockuso!"* (This is both a call to attention and a signal to begin the meditation period.) All students straighten their backs, place their hands on their laps, thumbs and fingers touching to form a circle, and close their eyes. Each student is responsible for clearing his mind of anything outside of the dojo and preparing himself mentally for the coming practice. After meditating for a short time, the senior student calls, *"Yame!"* to signal both the completion of the meditation period and the preparation for the *reis*, or bows. All eyes open, the master turns his body around so that he is facing the shrine and places his hands (first left, then right) on the floor in front of his knees. The senior student then calls *"Shomenirei,"* following which all bow at the waist in the deepest of respect. The master returns to face his students, whereupon the senior student calls out, *"Onegaishemasu,"* meaning "please teach me." All bow to the sensei. The sensei then returns the bow, bowing lower and more humbly than the rest.

After the bow, all students remain in their place waiting for the sensei to give instructions for the daily practice. It is very impolite to look down upon the sensei while he is in a sitting position. Also, no student should rise before the sensei has risen. The sensei rises first; then everyone follows and practice begins. When you rise from *seiza* to the standing position, you always bring your right leg up first, followed by your left. The samurai believed that the right side was the strong side and the left side was the weak. The origin of this belief is unknown, but if you look into the history of the samurai, you will find they were all right-handed. If you were female or not of samurai stock, then it did not matter if you were left-handed. To this day in Japan, the weak must always give way to the strong. The left side always touches the floor first when kneeling and is always the second to rise when standing. In most types of kata, whether the tea ceremony or a judo kata, the right foot is always in a protected position, never allowing shame to fall on the honorable right side.

It is a well-established custom in the traditional dojo that, if the master has taken the time to teach you personally, you must present yourself to him after the class and before he rises from his sitting position. This is accomplished by getting up from the ranks and approaching the master from the right side center, kneeling before him, keeping your head up, back straight, hands on thighs and awaiting his recognition of you. At such time, you will bow deeply and thank him for his time and apologize for your mistakes. After he has made his comments, he will return the bow and you will be free to leave. Pushing yourself backwards on your knees, at least twelve inches, it is now proper for you to stand and retire from the floor.

Discussions of dojos and senseis always cause me to remember when I was in Japan with my teacher. He was a 7th degree black belt and I was a *shodan*, or 1st degree black belt. He took me to where he trained and introduced me to his teacher, Yoshio Ohtsuka. I was incredibly excited about going to this very old dojo and training with a teacher who you read about in history books. Ohtsuka Sensei was then ninety-three years old, but he looked like a man of about fifty. Like most elderly Japanese, he was rather slightly built and had salt and pepper hair. His most discerning feature was his eyes; when he looked at you, he seemed to peer into your very soul.

We arrived at the dojo about 6:30 A.M. so that my teacher could get Sensei's permission for me to work out. I could tell, from the way he kept telling me things to do and not to do, that my teacher was nervous about taking me with him. But no matter what his feelings, he had made the decision to take me and now I was his responsibility. As we walked up the steps of the dojo, I remember thinking, "No matter what, I cannot afford to make any mistakes." I don't know if my sensei knew my level of knowledge about the Japanese way (perhaps that was why he was so nervous), but I knew that if I did anything wrong in the dojo, there would be no excuse; my teacher would have to accept the blame.

We took off our shoes and bowed as we entered the main hall. Sensei motioned for me to follow him down the corridor where we came upon a small sliding door. As he knocked, I could hear someone from inside say, "Just a moment please," followed in the same breath by, "Come in!" Sensei slid the door open and motioned for me to follow him. We got down on our knees upon entering. I watched as he pushed himself across the floor to a man who sat watching television with his back turned toward us. My teacher sat there very quietly while I waited at the door. We stayed like this, in our kneeling position, until the man finished his program; he then turned around and addressed Sensei. They exchanged the usual pleasantries. Sensei looked at me, saying I was his friend and asked for permission for me to work out. Without looking at me, but motioning for me to come forward, they continued their conversation. I pushed myself forward as I had seen Sensei do and reached the place where the two men were sitting. Sensei introduced me and I bowed deeply and humbly saying, "It is an honor to meet you." Reaching into my pocket, I presented a small gift to him and added, "Thank you for allowing me to practice with you today." With this, Sensei and I pushed ourselves backward toward the door. After we were outside, Sensei slid the door closed. We stood up and I followed him to the dressing room.

In the dressing room, there were many students hurrying about getting dressed. Sensei motioned me to a small corner where we changed, then proceeded to the practice floor and waited for the head instructor to enter. After everyone assumed their position on the floor in several straight, rigid lines, the head sensei entered and took his position in front of the class. The master was accompanied by his appointed aide, who hurried about attending to his needs and helped in preparing the class to begin. At this time, the head master bowed to the senior student, who in reply called out in a loud, clear voice, "*Mockuso!*" We all closed our eyes and relaxed into deep thought, trying to obtain a "no-thought" state of mind and mentally preparing ourselves for the upcoming lesson. In a few moments, the senior student called, "*Yame!*" After the formal bowing-in ceremony and after the master had risen from his position, all students hurriedly made a circle and began their warm-up exercises.

I will not go into detail about the warm-up or the lesson, but rather will tell of the event that occurred after the class. Adhering to custom, I prepared to give my thanks to the master for his personal instruction. My sensei had also instructed me to do just that. As I approached the master, he was talking to another student explaining some of the techniques demonstrated that day. I waited in a kneeling position, approximately eight feet in front of him and to his right. I could tell the master was aware of my presence but he had not indicated he was ready to receive me. So patiently I waited . . . and waited . . . and waited until my limbs had completely gone to sleep. I tried not to notice the clock on the wall, or my sensei, who sat perspiring, afraid that I might leave after making the commitment to the master. Forty-seven minutes had passed and still the master continued in conversation. I remember thinking that, no matter what happened, I was not going to allow myself or my teacher to be humiliated by abandoning the situation I had created. At 9:55 A.M., exactly fifty-two minutes from the time I approached the master, he excused the student in front of him and recognized me officially. I would like to note that neither the other student nor myself could move from our position without it being plainly obvious that we were in agony.

After being formally recognized, I pushed myself forward and bowed to the master. He returned the bow and then asked me what I had learned from the lesson. Decidedly humble, I responded, "Humility." I thanked him for my lesson and his patience and understanding. We exchanged bows and he quickly rose to his feet and left the floor. My teacher, who had been patiently pacing the perimeters of the dojo, came to my rescue as I attempted to rise. When I was unable to do so, Sensei laid me back on the floor and rubbed my legs vigorously to circulate the blood. After he helped me to my feet, I hobbled across the floor to the dressing room. We bathed, dressed, and left the fond, albeit painful, memories of a lesson well-learned: if one has the true desire for knowledge in the martial arts, once a commitment is made it must be fulfilled, regardless of the circumstances encountered.

My many return visits to this dojo always included thorough instruction, compassion, and respect. Due to the language barrier, the master always made sure that, before class was over, I had thoroughly understood the lesson of the day.

UNIFORM PROCEDURES: *UWAGI* AND *HAKAMA*

The jujitsu costume is referred to as a *gi*. It consists of two or three pieces of attire, depending on the dojo, and, in some cases, on rank. In many Japanese police dojos, the practice of taiho jitsu is done with the *hakama*, a divided, pantlike skirt. This is due to the fact that a tremendous number of taiho jitsu practitioners are also kendo students. My instruction in taiho jitsu has always been with men who were also Japanese elite kendo senseis and who wore the hakama.

Jujitsu can be practiced in the usual judo gi by itself or in the judo gi with the hakama worn over the gi pants *(zuban)*. The gi top, called *uwagi,* should be white or dark blue; likewise with the hakama. The karate gi is usually unsuitable because it is too lightly constructed and tears easily. The hakama allows complete movement: its large legs permit good air circulation when you are practicing the throws. My personal feeling about the uniform is simple. You can wear whatever you can afford and move comfortably in. After all, jujitsu is a street art. The hakama is merely the icing on the cake, to wear if you want to get the "samurai feeling."

Figure 1 shows how to fold your uwagi. Too often we see practitioners in the martial arts stuffing their uniforms into a bag. A good uniform is expensive; it can cost as much as $700 to $800, so treat it with respect.

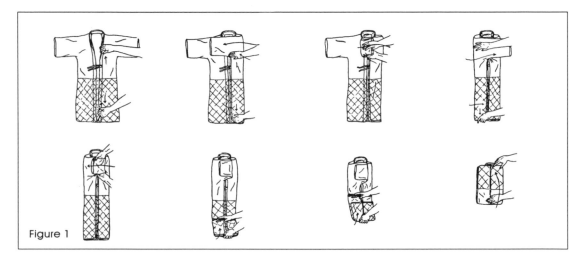

Figure 1

There are various ways (too numerous to describe here) to put on the hakama. Although it is considered by some to be excessively formal and outdated, my preference is reflected in Figure 2 and is described as follows. (a) Begin by stepping into the hakama with the stiffener (*koshi-ita*) to the back. (b) Pull the front up, take hold of the cords, wrap them behind you, and, changing hands, bring the cords to the front again. (c) Cross the

Figure 2

cords in front and about three inches down from the top waist band. (d) Pull them to the rear and tie them in a bow. Make sure that your top is pulled down tight so there is no bulge in the back. (e) Pick up the back of the hakama with both hands. Place the koshi-ita over the bow and bring the cords to the front. Drawings (c) and (f) show that all cords, front and back, are in line crossing to the front. Tie a small knot in the center where the cords cross. (g) Take one end and fold it back and forth across the knot, making all ends even. (h) Take the other end and circle it around the bow until no cord is left. When you finish, it should look like drawing (i), with no ends showing.

We will now discuss probably the most basic requirement of any martial art, yet one of the hardest subjects to convey to the beginner: *happo-no-kuzushi*, the directions of off-balance.

Figure 3   Figure 4

HAPPO-NO-KUZUSHI: Directions of Off-Balance

Throughout this book, we continually utilize the concept of *happo-no-kuzushi*. A frequently ignored and misunderstood concept, it is so fundamental to the art of jujitsu and the successful execution of its techniques that its importance cannot be overemphasized. Study it thoroughly until you have mastered it and understand its theory; otherwise you will find yourself confused and totally frustrated when you attempt the techniques.

We start first with the concept of a person's "working circle." The circumference of a working circle constitutes the farthest point a person can reach for defense—that is, with his arms or legs—without leaning. Each person's working circle will have a different circumference, depending on his height and the length of his legs. You can determine your circle by attaching (preferably by safety pin) one end of a $2^1/2$- to 3-foot string to the inseam of your gi pants. To the other end, attach a small weight. Now simply stand at attention, with your feet approximately 4 to 5 inches apart. Be sure to stand erect, with your back straight; do not lean forward or backward or to either side. You will now be what a plumber would describe as "plumb," or perfectly centered. Have someone take a piece of chalk and mark an X on the floor at the point above which the weight has come to rest, then remove the pin and the string. Place the center of your buttocks on the X and extend both legs straight out in front of you (see Figure 3).

While maintaining this position, have your partner place the chalk at your heels. Pivot on your buttocks with your legs extended until you have drawn a complete circle around your body. Stand up and straddle the X (see Figure 4).

Think of this circle as a large hula hoop. (If you do not know what a hula hoop is, one of your parents or grandparents can describe it to you.) To complete this explanation, we need four of these imaginary hoops. In Figure 5, we are standing in the center of the first imaginary hoop, with the second hoop around us from front to back. As shown on the happo-no-kuzushi chart (see Figure 8), this second hoop will allow you to utilize the front and back positions 1 and 5 (*mamae-no-kuzushi* and *maushiro-no-kuzushi*) for off-balancing.

Figure 6 shows a third imaginary hoop, which runs diagonally through us and utilizes off-balance positions 8 and 4 (*hidari-maesumi-no-kuzushi* and *migi-ushirosumi-no-kuzushi*). Figure 7 shows our fourth imaginary hoop, which also runs diagonally through us at a 90-degree angle to the third hoop and utilizes positions 2 and 6 (*migi-maesumi-no-kuzushi* and *hidari-ushirosumi-no-kuzushi*). I have intentionally left positions 3 and 7 (*migi-mayoko-no-kuzushi* and *hidari-mayoko-no-kuzushi*) off my samurai figure because, by now, you should have grasped the concept. If you have not, simply take Figure 5 and mentally turn the circle so that the hoop is from shoulder to shoulder rather than from front to back.

When you study Figure 8, keep in mind that these eight directions are the same off-balancing, or defending, directions used in all Japanese martial arts. Thus, if a Japanese martial artist asked you what the most important ingredient in your martial art was, and you replied "happo-no-kuzushi," he would probably smile slightly but be deeply impressed. Again, I cannot overemphasize the importance of recognizing and developing these eight directions of off-balancing.

Figure 4 reflects the most important and basic *mawai* in the happo-no-kuzushi theory. It indicates the farthest one can reach without running the risk of being knocked off balance. Years ago Sensei Tateno showed me a simple exercise to practice finding your mawai. You and your partner stand approximately 10 to 12 feet apart facing each other. Your partner will be the *uchidachi* (attacker) and you will be the *shidachi* (defender). On a given command, each person begins to walk slowly toward the other. When you feel he is about to step into your circle (as in Figure 4) shout "*Matte!*" and hold a hand directly in his face. This gives the verbal and visual command to "Stop." Now find your X as we described above and sit on it. Extend your feet as in Figure 3. If you have accomplished this exercise correctly, the uchidachi's forward toe should just touch one of your extended heels. If not, repeat the exercise until you get it right.

This exercise can also be used to find your arm mawai. Simply walk rapidly toward a wall and come to an abrupt stop when you feel that you've reached the correct mawai with your arms. Reach straight out and attempt to touch the wall with your fingertips. Do not adjust your feet or move your shoulders forward in any manner. You should be perfectly centered. Again, if you have done the exercise correctly, your fingertips will just touch the wall; if not, repeat it.

To utilize the happo-no-kuzushi theory, think of yourself as being inside a huge ball with no sides and no top or bottom. A ball simply spins when being confronted by any forceful object. Dr. Kano summarized this concept by stating, "Maximum efficiency with minimum effort."

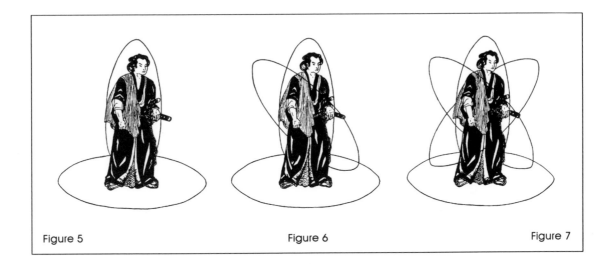

Figure 5   Figure 6   Figure 7

HAPPO-NO-KUZUSHI

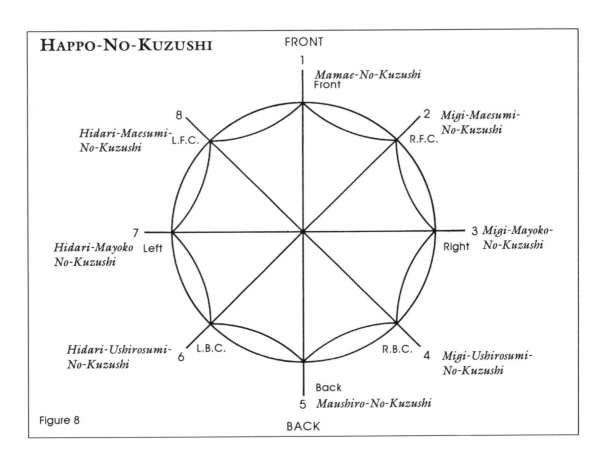

FRONT

1
Mamae-No-Kuzushi
Front

8
L.F.C.

Hidari-Maesumi-
No-Kuzushi

2 *Migi-Maesumi-*
No-Kuzushi
R.F.C.

7   Left
Hidari-Mayoko
No-Kuzushi

3 *Migi-Mayoko-*
No-Kuzushi
Right

L.B.C.
Hidari-Ushirosumi-
No-Kuzushi 6

R.B.C.
4 *Migi-Ushirosumi-*
No-Kuzushi

Back
5 *Maushiro-No-Kuzushi*

Figure 8

BACK

KAMAI: Postures

After mastering the happo-no-kuzushi, we can move on to the two basic postures, *migi-chudan-no-kamai* (Figure 9) and *hidari-chudan-no-kamai* (Figure 10). (*Migi* means right and *hidari* means left.) These two basic stances will be your starting position throughout the upcoming wazas. To assume them, visualize yourself standing in *shizen hontai* in the center of Figure 8; thus, your left foot will be on line 7 and your right foot will be on line 3. To assume hidari-chudan-no-kamai, your right foot stays in place. Step forward with your left foot one natural step, toes pointing straight ahead. Your left hand will come forward, fingers pointing straight ahead on line 1, throat high. Your right hand will also come on line 1, just behind your left hand and just above your navel. The migi-chudan-no-kamai is the exact reverse. Please read this procedure again carefully and assume the right and left forward postures.

Figure 9   Figure 10

There are numerous postures, but I will narrow them down to the five most commonly used, being five right and five left. Now follows a brief, but very important, exercise designed to assist you in moving from one posture to another, throughout the eight points. It is essentially a brief *ashi*, or foot, kata. When practicing these movements, be sure the rear heel never touches the floor. If you let it touch the floor, you will inevitably experience a backward motion, which is entirely unacceptable. Even though you are changing direction from right to left and forward and back, you should always feel that your body is moving forward.

To begin the exercise, place the happo-no-kuzushi chart on the floor in front of you so that the word "front" is to your front. Start in the migi-chudan-no-kamai. Leaving your right foot in place, move your left foot counterclockwise and behind your right foot. The center line of your left foot should now be on line 3. Your right knee should be slightly bent so that it is over your right big toe. Your hands will swing to your left accordingly. This is a defensive posture. Now let your right foot pivot counterclockwise until the toes are pointing toward line 7. Both feet are now pointing straight ahead and are approximately shoulder distance apart. To flow into the attack position, simply step forward with your left foot one normal step and shift your hands so that the left hand is forward and the right hand is to the rear. You will now be in the hidari-chudan-no-kamai defensive posture, which the Japanese refer to as *jigo hontai*.

Now, as if the chart were directly beneath you, pivot on the heel of your left foot clockwise so that the toes are pointing to the front (line 1). Move your right foot to your right, clockwise and behind your left foot. It will be slightly to the side of line 7, with the toes pointing at line 3. Bend your left knee so that it is over your left big toe and your rear foot is in line with your left heel, left hand forward and right hand to the rear.

To place yourself back in hidari-chudan-no-kamai, pivot on the ball of your left foot clockwise 90 degrees. Both feet are now pointing toward line 3, with the rear heel slightly off the floor ("thinking forward but not leaning forward"), so that you could slide a piece of paper under it. Step with your right foot one normal step straight ahead in the direction of line 3. Lift the heel of your left foot slightly. Your hands simultaneously change positions, so that your right hand is forward and your left hand is to the rear. You are now in the migi-chudan-no-kamai posture.

Look to your left and imagine the chart again as being in the center of your body. Leaving your right foot planted, bend your right knee to the front slightly, pivot your left foot 90 degrees counterclockwise, and then bend your right knee so that it is directly over your right big toe. Your left leg should come to rest on line 5. Your right foot is on line 3, your right hand is forward, and your left hand is to the rear. Your rear heel is slightly off the floor. You will be in migi-chudan-no-kamai, facing to the front. If you do this as explained, you should be looking at the words *happo-no-kuzushi*, with your right heel on the edge of line 1 and your right toes pointing to line 3. Your left foot should be on line 5, with your left toes pointing to the front. Again, your rear heel is up slightly; do not lean forward. If you find yourself losing your balance, simply lower your center of gravity by bending your knees a little more. Pivot on the ball of your right foot 90 degrees counterclockwise, step forward with your left foot one step, simultaneously reverse your hand positions and bring your right heel slightly off the floor. You will be in hidari-chudan-no-kamai.

Pivot on the heel of your left foot 90 degrees clockwise, left toes pointing at line 3 and heel at line 7. Step around and behind your left foot clockwise with your right foot. Bend your left knee as described above. You will now be facing line 5 in hidari-chudan-no-kamai. Pivot on the ball of your left foot, bringing the heel 90 degrees clockwise. Your left toes are pointing at line 5; your left heel is at line 1. Step with the right foot straight forward, and simultaneously reverse your hand positions. You will be in migi-chudan-no-kamai.

You are now facing to the back of the chart. Pivot on the heel of your right foot 90 degrees to your left. Your right toes will be pointing at line 3; your right heel at line 7. Swing your left foot all the way around, counterclockwise, to your left to line 5. Bend your front knee, keeping your left heel slightly off the floor. Your hands should move in accordance with your body movement. You will be facing toward the front of the chart in migi-chudan-no-kamai. Step forward with your left foot, allowing your right foot to pivot so that both feet are pointing toward the front, right heel slightly raised, hands in a hidari-chudan-no-kamai posture.

This concludes one half of the exercise. To practice the other half, simply pivot on your left foot and bring your right foot to the rear on line 7. You will be facing toward line 3 in a hidari posture. Proceed with the drill by reversing the above instructions.

How these eight points of off-balancing relate to the critical off-balancing process itself will be thoroughly addressed in Chapter Two.

NOTES

1. *Webster's Third New International Dictionary*, (Springfield, MA: G. & C. Merriam Co. Publishers, 1986).
2. Norris and Ross McWhiften, *1973 Guiness Book of World Records*, (New York: Bantam Books), p. 552.
3. Senta Yamada, *The Principles and Practice of Aikido* (New York: Arco Publishing Co., 1961), p. 12.
4. Oscar Ratti and Adele Westbrook, *Secrets of the Samurai*, (Boston and Tokyo: Charles E. Tuttle Co., Inc., 1973).
5. E. J. Harrison, *The Fighting Spirit of Japan*, (W. Foulsham & Co., undated; distributed in the United States by Sterling Publishing Co., New York).
6. Ibid.
7. Ibid.
8. H. Irving Hancock and Katsukuma Higashi, *The Complete Kano Jiu-Jitsu (Judo)*, (New York: Dover Publications, 1905). Note: Translated from the Japanese Kodokan Judo rules.
9. Ibid.
10. G. Koizumi, *My Study of Judo*, (New York: Sterling Publishing Co., 1960).
11. Peter Urban, *The Karate Dojo*, (Boston and Tokyo: Charles E. Tuttle Co., Inc., 1967).
12. Hokushinkan Chiba, Osaka, Japan.
13. Ibid.

> **"What we call 'I' is just a swinging door which moves when we inhale and when we exhale."**
>
> —Shunryu Suzuki
> *Zen Mind, Beginners' Mind*

CHAPTER TWO
Basic Self-Defense Techniques

I WANT to start what we could call the "instructional" part of this book with some basic self-defense techniques. Before we get involved in them, however, I'd like to make an observation about martial arts. At one time martial arts were taught mainly for protection. One studied with a teacher because of his reputation or his particular style. In today's society, we can't rely solely upon this trick or that to protect us, for everyone seems to have a gun. Rather, we should study martial arts today for perfection—of the mind, of the body, and of the spirit. Through endless effort of practice for perfection, you will find the ultimate in protection. As you practice these techniques, remember: it's not the art you must master as much as the discipline in the art. No one art is really better than the other. The practitioner makes the art, not the other way around.

Remember also that all martial arts are defensive. In karate, every kata starts with a block; in aikido, someone has to attack you to make the technique work; in judo, someone has to take hold of you or attack you. If a 10th degree black belt in judo and a 10th degree black belt in karate squared off to duel and all variables were equal, (such as age and weight), who would win? Some would say "karate," others would say "judo." But whoever said one or the other does not understand what I am trying to explain. The correct answer is simple: no one would win. There would not be a fight: if all things were equal, neither man would attack. If one did attack in such circumstances, he would surely lose, for the attack would create a weakness in the art.

With this thought in mind, let's turn our attention to some features common to all martial arts techniques. First, there are five critical ingredients to all techniques: timing, balance, posture, coordination, and speed. These five elements are required to correctly perform any technique. Second, there are three sequential components to any jujitsu technique:

1. *kuzushi*—balance, specifically what we call off-balancing the opponent while maintaining your own balance
2. *tsukuri*—entry into the technique
3. *kake*—execution of the technique

25

Most new students—and many not-so-new students who should know better—frequently want to omit kuzushi and immediately jump to kake. Like a person watching the magician, they think not about the hours of preparation it took to execute the illusion, but only about the illusion itself. You *must* follow the simple rule of performing these elements *in the order stated*. Thus, when practicing *every* technique in this book, you must first break the balance of your attacking opponent—whether he's kicking at you, grabbing you, or striking out at you—before proceeding to entry and execution of a technique. Once the balance is broken in a certain direction (we will explain that direction in its entirety by using the happo-no-kuzushi chart extensively), you may proceed to step 2: tsukuri. We will also explain entry by reference to the chart. If you follow these directions, you will conclude that step 3, the execution of the technique, is quite simple.

Even though we describe these three phases of any successful technique as "steps," it should not be inferred that there is a pause or interruption between each step when actually performing a technique. It is perfectly acceptable to do so occasionally when *practicing* in order to confirm that you have proper foot alignment, posture, hand position, and so on. But in the actual performance of a technique, the process from "step" to "step" must be fluid and continuous.

In executing these techniques, you must also understand the concept of your mechanical center—the region in which your body must pivot, be it the leg, the knee, the arm, or the elbow. Therefore, controlling these areas on the attacker should become your main objective. When you control these areas, you restrict the attacker's freedom. In moving your own body to achieve this control, your body movements (*tai-sabaki*) must be performed without weakening your stability.

Natural standing posture is called *shizen hontai*. It is upright and not strained; the feet are approximately shoulder distance apart. Correct posture is most important, for without it you will lose your balance. If you constantly lose your balance while practicing a technique, perhaps you are attempting to take your attacker off his balance incorrectly. Or perhaps you are standing too upright—that is, in a strained manner. Try lowering your center of gravity by bending your knees slightly. Your feet control your stability; thus, they should not be close together or widely separated, and they should not be crossed except when specifically called for in a technique. When you move one foot, be sure to point your toes, lift your knee, and relax the lower part of the leg. Doing so will allow your body weight to transfer slowly to the moved foot.

Remember that a properly executed technique always works. If a technique is not working for you, it is you, not the technique, that needs adjustment. In many of the old samurai training halls, there's a large sign just inside the door that states, "If you are having problems with a waza, return to the beginning." Most of us don't like to return to the beginning: it seems so far away. But it is always best to ask directions when you are lost. Don't wander around hoping to find something that looks familiar.

Each technique should be analyzed and studied in the following order:

1. variations of correct counters
2. involuntary and voluntary openings in the attack
3. technical theory—kuzushi, tsukuri, kake
4. counterattack—defenses
5. successive attack—*renzoku-waza*

It is not my intent to instruct you in the art of *ukemi*, for this art is of judo after 1882. Jujitsu, to my knowledge and Sensei Hata's knowledge, had no structured pattern of learning to fall. But I would like to emphasize the use of the "pat" signal. When someone is applying pressure to a joint or performing a choking technique (*shime waza*), there will come a point—most certainly directed by pain—when the uke will need to submit to prevent having a bone broken or being choked unconscious. Patting either the mat or the tori himself, twice in a rapid succession and hard enough for the tori to hear or feel, signifies to the tori to immediately let go. It is most important for tori to respond *immediately* to the uke's pat. It is not—I repeat, not—the tori's prerogative to decide for the uke how much pain the uke can withstand.

In today's society, we must have a reasonable way of training. The techniques in this book should be practiced in a semiformal manner, with a prearranged order of attack and defense. This enables the practice of techniques slowly or quickly, as desired, with complete control and without undue physical strain. As you become familiar with the techniques, you will be able to perform them singularly or in sets. In this book, we frequently use the terms *uke* and *tori*. *Uke* is the attacker or recipient of the technique; he provides openings to attack. *Tori* is the defender; he actually performs the techniques. The repetitive practice of one movement, even if it's just *ashi waza*, we call *uchi komi*. Some define it as "striking in." In old jujitsu terminology it is called *buttsukari*, meaning "crashing in."

We have reviewed all the important elements leading up to the actual attack and defense. Now let's come back to the beginning, *balance*. In breaking the attacker's balance, you must concentrate initially on his mind, then on his body. For instance, if you reach quickly toward someone's face, he will immediately move his head away from your hand. It's his subconscious at work. Another example: Each of us has sometime become so deeply involved in a project that everything else became a void. Suddenly, someone touched you or spoke your name. Subconsciously, you raised your hands toward your face, simultaneously moved away from the interruption, and stated something similar to, "Oh! You frightened me." What the other person did in that microsecond was, first, break your balance (when you leaned away) and, second, create an opening for attack (when you raised your hand to protect your face). These are subconscious reactions. In jujitsu, the object of breaking the attacker's balance is to force him to make a subconscious second move in the direction we wish to apply our technique.

For a more concrete example, let's once again look at the happo-no-kuzushi chart. Assume that my attacker and I are facing each other. He is standing in the center of the chart, facing line 1; I am at the top of the chart bestriding the "1." If I wish to throw him on line 1 (forward), I can simply push him backward slightly—that is, toward line 5. His first response will generally be one of two moves. First, he may simply lean backward without moving his feet. If so, the back of his head will be beyond his rear heel. Or, second, he will step backward and lean slightly to the rear. The choice he makes is immaterial. Unquestionably, his second response will be either to return to an upright position or to resist my push by stepping forward. Either action will make him vulnerable to being off-balanced to the front—that is, on line 1. If I want to off-balance him backward, I simply take hold of his wrist slightly, pull forward along line number 1, and be prepared for all of the above to happen in reverse. Similarly, to throw him on line 7, I simply first pull him slightly in the direction of line 3. To throw him on line 2, I first break his balance on line 6. Each line can be used by simply remembering the preparatory movement in the direction of the opposite numbered line.

This procedure is simply an application of Dr. Kano's principle: when pulled, yield; when pushed, give way. Never stop the attacker's force; change its direction so it can be utilized into your own attack. Approximately thirteen years ago, Hata Sensei gave me two outstanding examples of breaking the balance (see Figures 11A and 11B). (I would give recognition to these two senseis, but unfortunately Hata Sensei was not absolutely sure who they were.)

Figure 11A

Figure 11B

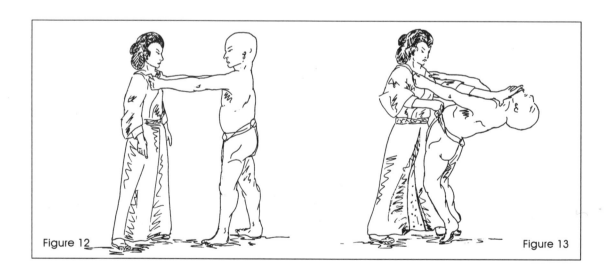

Figure 12

Figure 13

With the above in mind, let's now proceed to some actual techniques, both of which could have practical application on today's streets. In each, unless we state otherwise, tori will bestride the "1" of the happo-no-kuzushi chart, facing the center of the chart, (that is, the point at which the lines converge). Uke will bestride the center, with his right foot on line 3 and his left foot on line 7.

TECHNIQUE NUMBER 1:
Defending Against a Double Lapel Grab

In Figure 12 uke grips tori's lapels with both hands; in Figure 13 tori slides his left foot forward toward line 5. Tori's left foot should come to rest between uke's legs and just beyond his buttocks. Simultaneously, tori reaches with his left hand through uke's arms, placing the palm of his left hand on uke's chin while firmly grabbing his belt or waistband with his right hand. Tori pulls his right hand toward his solar plexus and pushes up and downward, in a "wave" motion, under uke's chin toward line 5. As uke loses his balance backward, tori concludes his attack in either of two ways. In one, he smashes his left elbow into uke's solar plexus with a straight up and down motion while simultaneously attacking uke's groin with his right knee. In the second, tori simply releases his grip. Uke will fall backward; tori then slides slightly forward with his left foot and kicks to uke's groin with his right foot.

TECHNIQUE NUMBER 2:
Defending Against a Rear Head Hold

In Figure 14 uke (who in this case is not bestriding the center) attacks from tori's right rear and grabs tori around the neck with his left arm. As he does, he steps slightly in front of tori. As tori is bestriding line 1, uke should be standing approximately on line 7. Keep in mind that this will enable uke to hit tori in the face with his right fist.

To break uke's balance, tori simply reaches across the front of uke's left thigh with his left hand and pinches uke's inner right thigh approximately half way between the knee and groin. Uke's immediate response will be to move either his knee or his foot to his

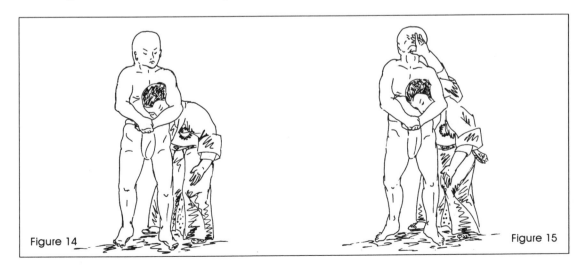

Figure 14   Figure 15

right. Simultaneously, tori reaches around and over uke's left shoulder with his right hand and places his second finger under his nose (Figure 15). Tori pushes upward with the inside of his finger. This will force uke's head up. Now tori breaks uke's balance backward toward line 1, removes his right foot from behind uke, and presses harshly straight down toward the floor with his finger. This will cause uke to fall straight down and to the rear. [*Note:* When applying this technique, be sure to place your finger directly under the nostrils and firmly on the cleavage of the upper lip, taking care to keep your thumb away from uke's mouth.]

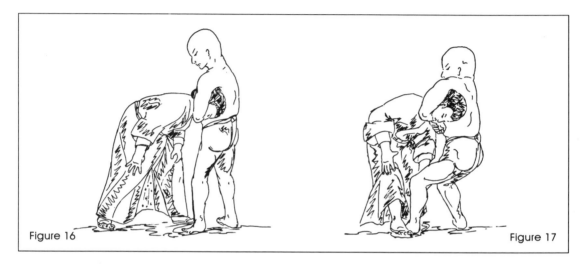

Figure 16   Figure 17

TECHNIQUE NUMBER 3:
Defending Against a Front Head Hold

As shown in Figure 16, this technique starts with tori striding line 1 and facing the front of the happo-no-kuzushi chart. Uke will be standing on line 7 and facing toward line 5. Uke's left arm is around tori's neck and under his chin. (Your first thought will probably be to try to strike uke's groin. But remember, in attack and defense, each person is allowed only one move before being countered by an opposite move. So, if you attack his groin, he probably will kick you in your groin or try desperately to break your neck. So let's get back to the technique and forget the "what if he does this" and/or "what if I do that.")

In Figure 17 tori places his right foot on uke's left foot. Simultaneously, he takes the palm of his left hand and strikes the side of uke's left knee toward line 3, at a 90-degree angle to tori's right. As uke loses his balance to his left, he will simultaneously try to counter by moving his right leg; he will be in a semisquatting position. Tori takes advantage of uke's subconscious movement and strikes uke's groin with his right hand, causing uke to fall on line 2.

TECHNIQUE NUMBER 4:
Defending Against a Kick to the Groin

In this waza (Figure 18), tori is standing in hidari-chudan-no-kamai with his right foot on or near line 1. Uke's right foot is approximately on line 4 and his left foot is on line 5.

In Figure 19 uke attacks with his left foot, trying to strike at tori's groin. As uke attacks, tori moves his right foot clockwise around and behind his left foot so it rests on line 2. Tori must be sure to bend his left knee so that it is over his left big toe, thus keeping his posture correct. Tori does not attempt to catch or stop uke's foot on its upward path; rather, he simply waits until uke's left leg starts its normal downward glide. This small pause takes *timing*. As uke's leg starts downward, tori brings his left hand with the palm up under uke's calf, thereby suspending uke's left leg in midair.

In Figure 20 tori now takes hold of uke's left ankle with his right hand, palm down, and allows his left hand to fall naturally to his side. Tori's hips and body are facing toward line 6. Tori steps with his right foot toward line 6, allowing his left foot to slightly pivot naturally, then brings his left foot forward and around and behind the calf of uke's supporting right leg. Tori's left leg should thus stop in the vicinity of line 4. [*Note:* As uke loses his balance backward, he will probably try to grab tori to help break his fall.] Tori simply lifts his left leg up and to his left rear, causing uke to land on the back of his head. This fall can be devastating. Sensei Takshi Kushida remarked about such falls: "I no need mat. Uke needs mat." (See Chapter Three for more about Sensei Kushida.) Remember to be compassionate with your uke; if you are not, you may run out of ukes.

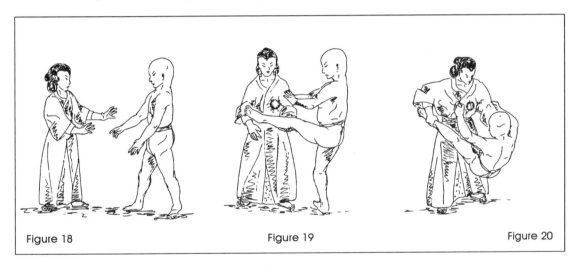

Figure 18   Figure 19   Figure 20

TECHNIQUE NUMBER 5:
Defending Against a Kick to the Groin
(*Mae-Geri-Keage-Hiza-Nage*)

As shown in Figure 21, tori is standing in migi-chudan-no-kamai. Uke is facing him and straddling line 5, with his right foot forward.

Figures 22 and 23 show uke attacking with his left foot; tori drops his hands slightly and pivots his left foot to the rear and behind his right foot, stopping on line 7. Tori's right knee is over his right big toe. Again, tori does not attempt to catch uke's foot on the upswing; rather, as uke's foot misses and starts its descent, tori pivots on the ball of his right foot so that his toes are now pointing toward line 3. Tori extends his right hand under uke's leg and catches it, simultaneously moving his left foot forward to where it is parallel with his right.

In Figure 24 tori then takes hold of uke's ankle with his left hand over the top.

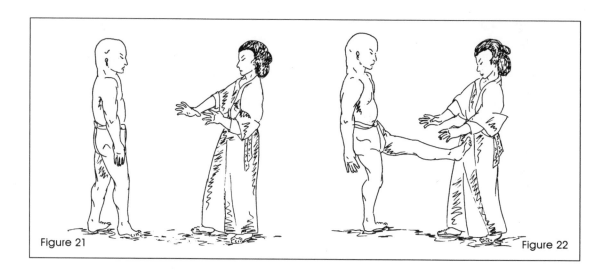

Figure 21

Figure 22

Figure 23

Figure 24

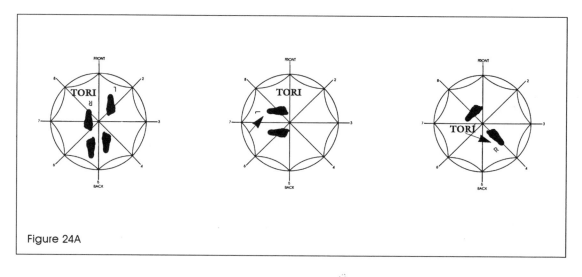

Figure 24A

Taking advantage of uke's off-balance, which will be backward to line 5, tori takes his right foot and steps across in the direction of line 4. He lifts his leg so that the back of his right calf is just above uke's right knee. Tori pulls his left hand towards him and pushes with his right hand toward line 2, while twisting his upper body to his left slightly. This will cause uke to fall on line 2.

Figure 24A reflects the happo-no-kuzushi diagrams for Technique Number 5.

After becoming familiar with this waza, you can lower your attacking leg below uke's knee and, with a sweeping upward motion, force uke's leg totally off the ground. This is a very dangerous and difficult fall for uke. Whether you push him gently or sweep partially, uke still has to fall facedown and in the direction of line 4.

Figure 25

Figure 26

TECHNIQUE NUMBER 6:
Defending Against a Front Grab, Preparatory to a Kick

In Figure 25 uke and tori are again standing in the same position as in the previous technique. As uke steps slightly forward with his right foot and attempts to grab tori with his right hand above his breast, tori steps forward with his right foot to line 6. Simultaneously, tori pushes up on uke's elbow with his right hand while placing his left hand on the outside of uke's right knee. Tori is thus in an extended low right stance.

While remaining in this stance, tori slides his left hand down to uke's ankle and immediately places his right hand on the inside of uke's right knee, as shown in Figure 26. Tori gives a pull/push motion—that is, pulls with his left hand and pushes with his right hand. Uke will lose his balance and fall in the direction of line 4.

TECHNIQUE NUMBER 7:
Defending Against a Kick to the Midsection

This technique starts with tori's back to the front of the happo-no-kuzushi chart, his right foot on line 1. Tori's left foot is in the normal position beside his right foot.

Figure 27

Figure 28

Figure 29

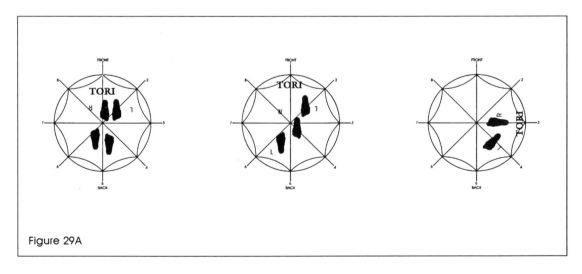

Figure 29A

Uke faces tori, straddling line 5, and attacks with his right foot, a kick to tori's midsection. As this happens, tori steps slightly to his left on line 3, and blocks the leg with his right hand (Figure 27).

In Figure 28 tori immediately steps to line 4 with his left foot and reaches around and in front of uke's neck with his left hand, allowing his right foot to pivot naturally toward line 7. His right hand takes hold of uke's right leg just under but in front of the knee. As tori pushes with his left hand in a downward direction, uke usually will panic and try to grab tori's body to regain his balance.

Tori continues pushing with his left hand so that uke's head is pointing at line 4 (Figure 29). When this is accomplished, tori bends his knees so that they are over his big toes, lifts with his right arm, and pushes down with his left arm. Uke will fall across tori's left thigh. This technique can be taken one step further by simply dropping down on your right knee as you lift with your right arm and dropping the attacker on your left knee. This makes it possible to break the attacker's back. *Be careful!*

Figure 29A shows the happo-no-kuzushi diagrams for this technique.

Figure 30   Figure 31   Figure 32

TECHNIQUE NUMBER 8: Defending Against a Kick to the Midsection (*Mae-Geri-Juji-Uke-Migi-Maki*)

This technique starts with tori's feet parallel with each other. Uke is facing to the front, bestriding line 5, in a left forward stance. Uke attacks with his right foot to tori's midsection. Tori immediately steps forward with his left foot to line 4 and uses an X block on the attacking shin as shown in Figure 30.

[*Note:* In utilizing the X block, the fists are tightly clenched to avoid injury and are thrust downward to strike just in front of uke's right ankle. The right hand should be over the left, palms facing down, elbows locked so they can withstand a strong kick. Do not lean the upper part of your body forward; to do so will weaken your kuzushi. The drawing shows uke's leg fully extended; it may be better to catch the leg while the knee is still slightly bent, so that uke's kick will not reach full force.]

Once tori has stopped the forward motion of uke's leg, he immediately slides his

Figure 33   Figure 34

right hand down and takes hold of uke's heel. Tori pulls his hands toward his chest with a clockwise motion (Figure 31). Uke's left foot will pivot so that tori's left hand is now holding the top of uke's right foot. While these movements are in process, tori slides his left foot slightly forward so that he is in a more upright position. These movements will force uke off balance on line 6.

As tori continues to pull toward his chest with his right hand, he places the top of uke's right foot in the crevice of his left elbow (Figure 32). Simultaneously, he slides his right hand to the back of uke's right knee. Tori then brings his right leg forward and strikes the back of uke's left supporting leg with the edge of his right foot. Uke will still be off balance toward line 6. [*Note:* When you are moving your right leg into the attack, allow your left foot to pivot naturally to your left; your body will follow.]

As uke continues to fall forward, tori keeps the pressure on the back of uke's left knee with his right foot (Figure 33). Tori places his right hand on uke's lower back and pushes downward. Figure 34 shows the completion of this technique. Tori can simply hold uke to the ground or remove his right foot while lifting slightly upward with his left arm and kick with his left foot to uke's groin.

TECHNIQUE NUMBER 9: Defense Against a Two-Handed Rear Wrist Grab (*Ryote-Dori*)

In this waza, both uke and tori are facing to the front, as shown in Figure 35. Tori has his right foot on line 3 and his left foot on line 7. Uke is standing directly behind tori, striding line 5; both are in a left-forward stance. (Keep in mind that everything will be reversed if you're in a right-forward stance.) Uke seizes both of tori's wrists.

In Figure 36, tori gives a gentle pull with his right hand forward and down toward line 2. This pull will cause uke to react subconsciously and pull back with his right hand, but his balance will have already been broken toward line 2. When this action occurs, tori immediately steps to his rear with his left foot to line 6. Simultaneously, he lifts his left hand straight up over his head.

Figure 37 shows the conclusion of this technique. Tori simply brings his right foot parallel to his left, bringing uke's left arm forward and stopping about chest high. Tori

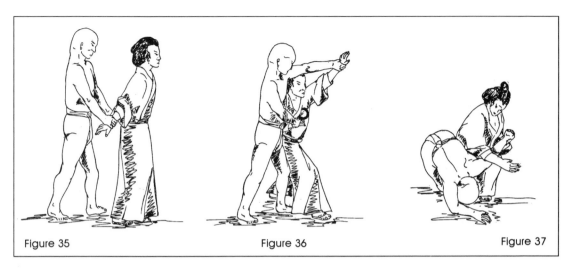

Figure 35　　　　　　　　　　Figure 36　　　　　　　　　　Figure 37

takes hold of uke's left wrist with his left hand. (Your right hand should break loose easily by prying against uke's thumb.) Bringing his right hand around behind uke's left arm, tori steps forward with his right foot to line 1, while applying pressure with his elbow or forearm to uke's left elbow. Tori goes down on his left knee. Uke will still be off balance toward line 2.

TECHNIQUE NUMBER 10:
Defending Against a Strike or Grab

[*Note:* Some of my technique titles use Japanese terminology; others are simply descriptions of defenses against this or that. The reason for this inconsistency is that either I was never told the Japanese term for the technique, or I forgot it, or there isn't a formal title. If the inconsistency really bothers you, by all means give the techniques names.]

This technique starts with uke and tori facing each other. Uke is bestriding line 5 and tori is bestriding line 1. Uke steps forward with his left foot and either strikes at or reaches for tori with his left hand. Tori steps with his right foot to the center of the happo-no-kuzushi chart and blocks with his left hand, palm open, to uke's wrist, as shown in Figure 38.

In Figure 39 tori takes hold of uke's left wrist, lifts uke's arm upward, and simultaneously pivots on the balls of his feet 180 degrees counterclockwise. Tori brings uke's left arm, elbow pointing down, to rest on tori's left shoulder. Tori is now facing the front of the chart and uke's left palm is facing upward. Tori now slides his left front foot slightly backward so that he has proper posture and balance, while pulling downward with uke's wrist toward tori's left knee. This will automatically bring uke off balance toward the front. Immediately tori executes a right elbow strike to uke's solar plexus.

In Figure 40 tori steps back with his right leg around and to the rear of uke's left leg; tori's right leg thus comes to rest on line 6. Simultaneously, tori pushes against uke's neck with his right forearm and elbow toward line 6. As uke loses his balance, he will probably try to recapture it by taking a small step to the rear with his right foot and trying to grab tori's forearm. To counter this move, tori simply bends his knees forward so that each knee is over its respective big toe, and pushes straight down with his right

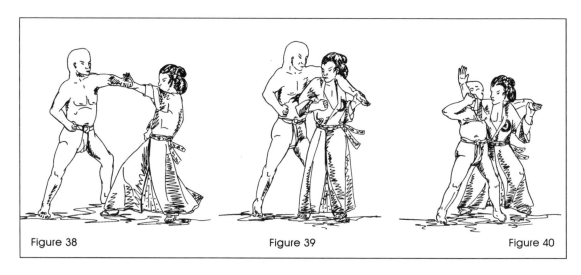

Figure 38   Figure 39   Figure 40

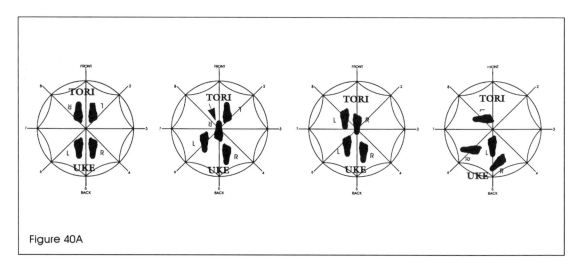

Figure 40A

forearm. This will cause the small of uke's back to land across tori's right knee. Figure 40A shows the happo-no-kuzushi diagrams for this technique, including the starting position.

TECHNIQUE NUMBER 11:
Defending Against a Front Bear Hug

In Figure 41 uke holds tori just above the elbows in a front bear hug.

In Figure 42 tori immediately brings his right knee to uke's groin.

As he feels this excruciating pain, uke will bend forward, lean forward, or otherwise have his balance broken forward. Before tori entirely removes his knee from uke's groin, he brings his right foot around to the outside, then places it on the floor behind uke's right leg (Figure 43). With his right hand, tori either reaches to uke's left bicep or simply pushes him in the face. Tori then takes hold of uke's right hand with his left hand and throws with a right *osoto gari*.

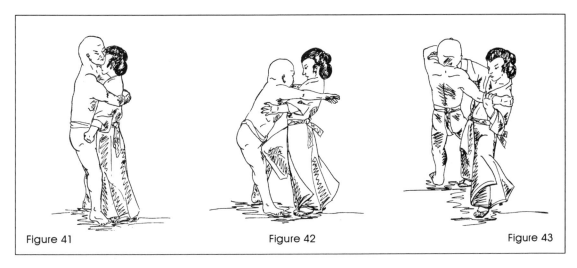

Figure 41   Figure 42   Figure 43

TECHNIQUE NUMBER 12:
Defending Against a Front Bear Hug

Figure 44 shows basically the same situation as in the previous technique. This time, however, uke has grabbed under tori's arms. The first movement in this waza cannot be shown clearly (Figure 45), so read this part very carefully. As uke squeezes tightly, tori places his left thumb and forefinger between uke's legs in the vicinity of the scrotum and *pinches!* [*Note:* Usually you pinch the tender skin between the testicles and the inner thigh. When you practice this once or twice, you'll realize just how tender this area is. If you pinch the inside of uke's left thigh, he'll move his left leg; if you pinch the inside of his right thigh, he'll move his right leg. You can also just pinch the top of either thigh.] In this particular technique, tori pinches the inside of uke's right thigh, then moves his right leg around and to the outside of uke's right leg. Then he simply places his right foot on the back side of uke's right knee and stomps straight down. [*Note:* You can take this waza one step further by simply pushing uke backward with your right hand.]

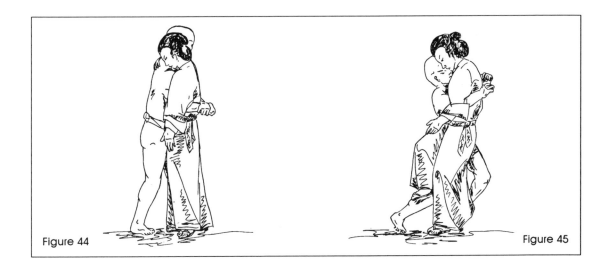

Figure 44   Figure 45

Figure 46

Figure 47

Figure 48

Figure 49

Figure 50

Figure 51

TECHNIQUE NUMBER 13: Defending Against a Two-Handed Front Wrist Grab (*Migi Ryote-Dori*)

This technique starts with uke and tori facing each other. Tori is bestriding line 1 and uke is bestriding line 5. This whole technique starts and ends on one line. Uke seizes tori's right wrist with both hands from the top. Tori steps with his left foot to line 2 while bringing his right forearm up parallel with the floor (Figure 46). Tori's feeling is one of pushing his elbow toward uke and pulling his wrist to his solar plexus.

In Figure 47 tori's movement will off-balance uke to uke's right. Subconsciously, uke pulls back on tori's wrist. The second that tori feels uke's resistance, he slides forward with his right foot followed by his left foot along line 6. Tori brings his right hand and both of uke's hands to the front, over the top of uke's head and finally to rest on the back of uke's neck. Uke will now be off balance backward. [*Note:* You can conclude this technique by simply pulling straight down, thereby forcing uke to let go of your wrist and falling on his back. Alternatively, while uke is in the process of falling, you may strike his groin with your left fist.]

TECHNIQUE NUMBER 14: Defending Against a Strike or Grab (*Empi Maki Kumade*)

In Figure 48 tori and uke are again standing as at the beginning of the previous technique—that is, facing each other in *shizentai*, bestriding lines 1 and 5, respectively. As uke steps forward with his left foot and reaches out to seize tori with his left hand, tori takes a slight step forward with his right foot and strikes the inside of uke's left forearm with the outside of his right wrist. This will bring uke off balance slightly in the direction of line 8.

Tori moves his right arm under and to the outside of uke's forearm, placing his open hand on uke's elbow. Once this is accomplished, tori pushes slightly against the elbow to his left, breaking uke's balance to uke's right. Once he has broken uke's balance, tori closes his right fist, turns the palm toward himself, and starts a pressured sliding motion along uke's left forearm to uke's left wrist (Figure 49). As he does so, tori steps with his left foot to his left rear on line 2, followed slowly by his right foot.

As uke loses his balance to his right (Figure 50), it forces him to take a step toward line 2. Whether uke steps with his right or his left foot, tori continues applying pressure downward with his right forearm. Tori has now locked uke's wrist and forearm into the crevice of tori's right arm. As uke leans forward, tori simultaneously steps with his left foot in the direction of line 6 behind uke's left leg and strikes uke's chin vigorously with his left palm. As uke loses his balance backward in the direction of line 6, the back of his head will be over and beyond his buttocks, thus exposing his Adam's apple. With the edge of his left hand, tori strikes uke's Adam's apple.

Figure 51 is a reverse angle view of the conclusion of this technique.

TECHNIQUE NUMBER 15: Defending Against a Two-Handed Rear Wrist Grab (*Empi Nage*)

This technique begins with uke and tori both facing toward the front of the happo-no-kuzushi chart, as shown in Figure 52. Uke has tori by the wrists from behind. Uke's left foot is forward. (It is important to look behind you to see which foot your attacker has forward. The technique must be done from the same side as the forward foot. If his feet are parallel to one another, the direction of the technique does not matter.) Tori is standing in the center of the happo-no-kuzushi chart. His left foot is on line 7 and his right foot is on line 3.

In Figure 53 tori moves his right foot clockwise to line 6, allowing his left elbow to bend behind him, and naturally pivots his left foot. Tori takes hold of uke's left wrist with his left hand, simultaneously squatting so that his knees are over his big toes. Tori

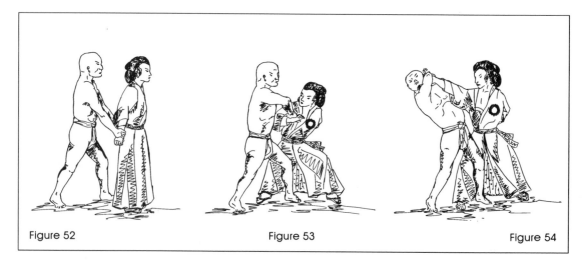

Figure 52   Figure 53   Figure 54

strikes uke in the solar plexus with his right elbow, turning his head to look directly at uke as he does so.

With this strike, uke's balance will be broken backward toward line 5 (Figure 54). As uke loses his balance, tori raises his right hand straight up and seizes uke's right wrist from the bottom. He swings it over uke's head and behind his neck, pushing straight down on the back of uke's neck with tori's own right forearm. This allows tori to throw uke over his right thigh. (In Figure 54, we have not taken the technique to the full extension as above mentioned.) After the elbow strike, tori simply raises uke's hand up to seize the inside of his wrist, strikes uke's jaw with his own wrist, and then throws him over his right thigh.

TECHNIQUE NUMBER 16: Defending Against a Grab, Push, or Strike (*Kuzure Hiza Guruma*)

Figure 55 shows this very simple but effective technique. Uke is standing facing tori. Uke's right foot is forward. Uke reaches out to grab, take hold of, push, shove, and so forth, tori. Tori takes the heel of his left foot and slams it into the back of uke's right knee.

Figure 55

As uke loses his balance in any direction, tori simply slams his right palm into uke's chest, thus throwing him down.

TECHNIQUE NUMBER 17: Defending Against a Front Grab, Preparatory to a Strike (*Ten Ken*)

This technique begins with tori's back to the front of the happo-no-kuzushi chart (as shown in Figure 56), uke grabs tori's left lapel with his right hand and begins a strike to tori's face with his left hand. Uke's right foot is forward.

In Figure 57, uke pulls with his right hand, tori seizes uke's right wrist with his right hand (as seen also in Figure 56) and turns it clockwise. Tori keeps uke's hand tight against tori's chest and simultaneously steps with his left foot to line 3, pivoting slightly so that he will be facing line 6. Tori takes uke off-balance on line 7 by striking the back of uke's elbow with his left forearm.

Figure 58 shows the conclusion of the technique. Tori simply steps forward on line 8 with his left foot. He takes hold of uke's right elbow with his left hand and forces him to the ground face first.

Figure 56   Figure 57   Figure 58

Please keep in mind when applying the wazas described in this book that they involve a tremendous amount of pain, besides the chance of breaking bones or rupturing arteries. Be sure your partner understands about "patting out" as a sign to stop *immediately.* As previously pointed out, it is not the prerogative of the person applying the technique to decide how much pain his partner can endure. But it is that person's responsibility to assure the safety and the well-being of his partner. Therefore, when uke signals by patting twice loudly on himself or, better yet, on tori, tori *must* immediately and spontaneously release his partner. As I wrote in *Iai, The Art of Drawing the Sword*:

> *From the viewpoint of purely technical skill, the beginner and the master are the same. All knowledge is a circle, for both the master and the beginner move instinctively without any cognition between perception and correct response. Once the first technique is learned, then the student is no longer a beginner and he is on the way. He must either continue to travel the circular path that is the way or he finds that he would have been better off if he had never learned his first technique.*[1]

With the conclusion of *ten ken*, we have come to the end of Chapter Two. In Chapter Three, we will learn about *te waza*, hand techniques.

NOTES

[1] Darrell M. Craig, *Iai, The Art of Drawing the Sword* (Boston and Tokyo: Charles E. Tuttle Co., Inc., 1981).

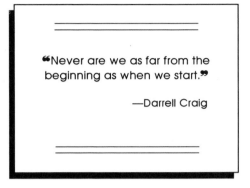

"Never are we as far from the beginning as when we start."

—Darrell Craig

CHAPTER THREE
Te Waza

ON ONE OF my trips to Japan, I had the pleasure of being escorted by the police to the Tokyo Yoshinkan Dojo, which is located just outside the metropolitan area where Sensei Gozo Shioda, 9th Dan Hanshi, is the director of the Yoshin style of aikido. Sensei Shioda studied directly under Sensei Morihei Ueshiba, founder of modern day aikido. Sensei Shioda not only is the founding father of the Yoshin style of aikido but is the chief instructor for his art in the Tokyo Metropolitan Police Department. Unfortunately, when I visited, Sensei Shioda was on a training maneuver with a police class, but I did have the opportunity to view a class. It was the closest to representing aikijitsu that I have ever seen; the demonstration was outstanding. It seemed as though every student was bandaged from head to toe. My understanding through an interpreter is that young police officers train for one year at this dojo. They then disperse to their own units to teach or help instruct in Sensei Shioda's art. I would highly recommend that any law enforcement person wanting to train in a hard style of aikido look into this style.

After returning home, I corresponded with the Yoshinkan office. It, in turn, got in touch with one of their outstanding instructors, Sensei Takshi Kushida, who has a dojo in the United States. The Yoshinkan office asked him to come to Houston to conduct a clinic at my dojo and a demonstration at the Houston Police Academy. His teaching and demonstration were probably the finest I have ever had the pleasure to witness and to participate in. I would like to say that I learned a lot from this sensei, but I can only say that I saw a lot, remembered some, and learned a little. He was positively dynamic. His teaching began with a short lecture. Then—presumably on some prearranged signal—his uke leapt to his feet and charged full speed at the sensei, who had his back to the attacking uke. We were all flabbergasted. To our astonishment, just as uke was about to strike Sensei, Sensei turned and, with a kiai and his forearm, struck uke about neck-high lifting his feet completely off the mat and forcing his body to become horizontal. As the dust settled and uke quickly retreated (we thought he had been killed), Sensei Kushida turned back to his openmouthed audience and stated simply, "I no need mat. Uke needs mat. Stand up and get your partner."

The techniques discussed in this chapter will be generally familiar to most aikido practitioners. Although the number of techniques is finite, there are numerous ways to demonstrate them.

Please keep in mind as you practice these techniques that you will not always be grabbed or seized as these drawings indicate. Thus, in an attack, you will very likely be working with a *kuzure* of (a part of) a *waza*; consequently, you must have what the Japanese call *nesshin*, "zeal in your method of practice." The technique must become a subconscious reaction to the uke's attack, with no thought of how the uke will attack or what technique you will use if he does this or that. If you wait for your mind to tell your body what to do, it will most likely be too late. Hata Sensei once told me that if something goes wrong while applying the technique, but you have broken the uke's kuzushi and your attacking movement is continuous (that is, without stalling), you most likely will succeed.

Do not become upset if you cannot make jujitsu techniques work the way you think they should. You must practice diligently three or four years before you can become semi-proficient. You don't have to be a dan grade in the art to achieve proficiency, but if you wish to gain depth in any art, you must seek a qualified teacher. This reminds me of an old Persian proverb:

> *He who knows not, and cares not that he knows not, is a fool—shun him.*
> *He who knows not, and knows that he knows not, is a child—teach him.*
> *He who knows, and knows not that he knows, is asleep—wake him. He who knows, and knows that he knows, is wise—follow him.*
>
> —Author Unknown

When you practice, always work with both sides, *migi* and *hidari*, in a *kumi-no-kata* manner. If you have difficulty with your left side, it is most likely because you are right-handed, like the majority of the world's population. Develop your proficiency with your weak side by performing routine functions such as drinking, cutting food, and putting on your shoes with your left hand. Try writing your name with your left hand (or vice versa for left-handed people). If you exercise throughout the day with your left hand, you will become fully ambidextrous for the first time in your life. Shortly after I began practicing this way, I stopped at a shop for a cup of coffee. While working on some papers I had brought with me, I started to reach for the cup with my right hand and then noticed that I already had the cup in my left hand. I was getting ready to pour it in my lap! This is when I first realized that all the practice I had been doing with the right side of my brain—by utilizing my left hand—was now producing results. This is not to say that your weak side will ever catch up to your strong side, but wouldn't it be advantageous to be able to use both hands and feet with similar precision?

> *You must believe me when I tell you that there are no short cuts in jujitsu. Each person entering into the art must labor in slow pain, like a mother giving birth. Only after the birth of her child can she explain the highs and lows of it.*[1]

Figure 59   Figure 60

TECHNIQUE NUMBER 1: (*Tenchi Nage*)

In Figure 59, uke and tori are facing one another; tori is facing toward the center of the happo-no-kuzushi chart. Uke's left foot is forward; tori's right foot is forward. Uke grabs tori's wrists.

Tori opens his hands so that his fingers are spread as far apart as possible. He then points the fingers of his left hand toward the ground and steps with his left foot to line 3, breaking uke's balance toward line 4 and to the rear. As tori steps with his left foot, he keeps uke's right arm straight. As shown in Figure 60, he then steps with his right foot to uke's right side (line 4). Simultaneously, he lifts uke's left arm above and behind his head. [*Note:* As tori steps with his right foot, he may apply *osoto gari kuzure*. To use this throw, he must get as close to uke as possible. He moves his left foot just behind uke's right foot and supports his entire body on his left leg. He raises his right leg approximately 6 to 8 inches off the floor and sweeps uke's legs out from under him. Tori should keep pushing uke backward with his right hand while holding uke's left wrist.] Tori can also convert this technique into *yoko tai otoshi* by simply placing his right leg all the way across uke's right side. Tori's heel will be in back of uke's right Achilles tendon. Tori forces the throw with his hands toward line 3.

TECHNIQUE NUMBER 2: (*Gaeshi Waza*)

This technique begins exactly the same as the previous technique. Tori pulls down and slightly out with both hands, breaking uke's balance forward and forcing him to take a small step forward with his left foot to counterbalance himself. (If you execute this movement correctly, uke will immediately respond by slightly pushing forward toward line 1.) As shown in Figure 61, tori takes advantage of uke's off-balance forward by stepping with his right foot across and in front of uke's right knee to line 3. While facing line 3, tori goes down on his left knee on line 7, lifting straight upward with his right hand. Simultaneously, tori takes hold of uke's right wrist with his left hand and pulls toward himself. This forces uke to fall forward toward line 2 and over tori's right leg. You may finish this waza by striking uke in the neck with your right fist after he has landed.

Figure 61

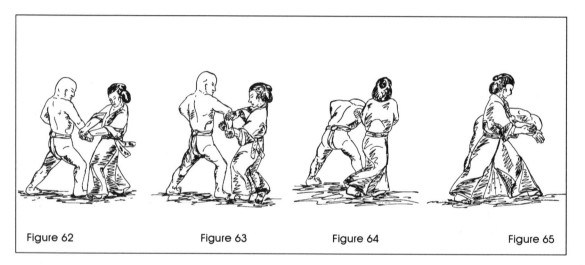

Figure 62 Figure 63 Figure 64 Figure 65

TECHNIQUE NUMBER 3: (*Ude Garami Nage*)

This waza starts out with tori's back to the front of the happo-no-kuzushi chart. Uke steps forward with his right foot and tries to seize or push tori with his right hand (Figure 62). Tori immediately blocks uke's right wrist with an X block downward, right hand over left, while stepping with his left foot to line 2. Tori steps to the outside of but parallel to uke's right foot.

In Figure 63, tori slides his right hand up to uke's elbow and pulls slightly toward line 8. Simultaneously, tori steps with his right foot to line 2, aligning his right foot to his left heel. The toes of his left foot will still be pointing to line 5. Tori bends his left knee so that it is approximately over his left big toe. This position will resemble Photograph 14 except that his left foot will be pointed forward.

While this is taking place, tori slides his left hand up and places it on uke's right shoulder blade (Figure 64). Things will now move very rapidly. Tori keeps pressure on uke's right elbow with his left hand, pivoting on the heel of his left foot so that his toes are pointing toward line 7.

Tori brings his right foot clockwise to line 4. Taking uke off balance on line 1, tori pivots on the heel of his left foot again. The toes of his left foot will now be pointing toward line 1.

In Figure 65, tori's left hand comes off of uke's shoulder blade and comes to rest between his shoulder and his elbow. Tori pushes down with his wrist on the back of uke's forearm and throws in the direction of line 1.

Figure 66   Figure 67   Figure 68

TECHNIQUE NUMBER 4: (*Morote Hasimi Kansetsu*)

This technique begins with tori's back to the front of the happo-no-kuzushi chart (Figure 66). Uke seizes tori's right wrist with his right hand. Uke and tori have their right feet forward.

In Figure 67, uke lashes out with his left hand to tori's face. With his left hand, tori blocks across his body and to the outside of uke's left wrist, while taking hold of the inside of uke's right wrist with his right hand. At this point, uke's off-balance will be slightly toward line 2, off of his right little toe.

In Figure 68, tori takes hold of uke's left wrist and pulls slightly toward line 2, while turning uke's left wrist clockwise so that the palm faces upward. Tori places uke's left elbow (which should be pointing down) into uke's right elbow joint, thereby locking the elbows together. Tori then steps with his left foot behind his right foot, aligning his left toes with his right heel. He bends his right knee and throws toward line 2. If you wish to break the elbow, simply straighten your right foot so the toes will be pointing toward line 3 and, with your left hand, pull uke's left wrist toward line 7. The actual footwork shown in Figure 68 is of the elbow break.

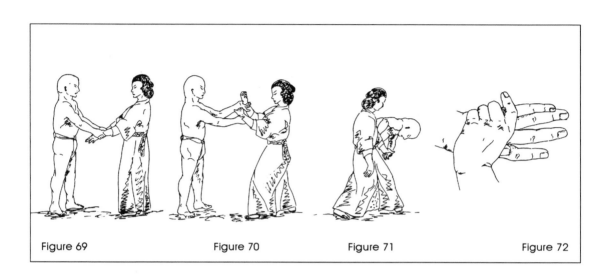

Figure 69   Figure 70   Figure 71   Figure 72

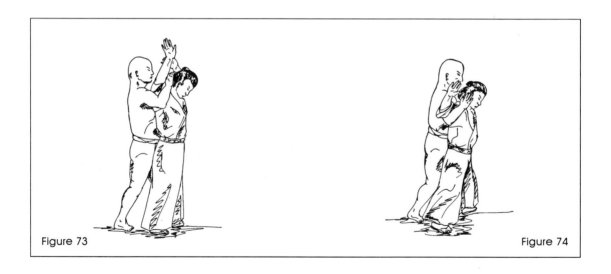

Figure 73   Figure 74

TECHNIQUE NUMBER 5: (*Kuzure Kote Gaeshi*)

In Figure 69, tori has his back to the front of the happo-no-kuzushi chart, with his left foot forward. Uke seizes tori's wrists. Tori pulls downward with both arms toward his knees, causing uke to take a step forward with his left foot.

    The off-balancing of uke by tori's forward motion allows tori to take a step toward line 5 with his left foot (Figure 70). While rotating his right hand clockwise, palm facing himself, tori reaches under uke's left wrist and takes hold of the inside of uke's thumb with his left hand. While this is taking place, tori moves his right foot behind his left, clockwise to line 4, bending his left knee and throwing uke on line 8 (Figure 71). Figure 72 shows a close-up of the hand position.

TECHNIQUE NUMBER 6: Full Nelson (*Mochi*)

One of the most well-known holding techniques is generally referred to as a full nelson (Figure 73). Although this technique is sometimes difficult to get out of, it is also one of the most difficult to apply. Frequently, if you tell someone you study martial arts, he will tell you that he has a hold from which you cannot escape. He then gets behind you, asks you to lift your arms and applies the full or half nelson. Once he gets you in the full nelson, only one of two things can happen. One, you're going to hurt him and lose a friend. Or, two, you will not be able to escape. So I suggest that when he steps around behind you and reaches under your arms, just take hold of your belt or obi at each hip, keeping your elbows tight to your sides. You must use, as the Japanese say, *genki* and take a *fusegi* posture. Your friend will not be able to get his hands up and behind your neck as long as you keep your elbows tight to your sides and you maintain a firm grip on your obi. Usually, he will then say, "Well, let me get hold of you first." You should quickly answer, "I thought you were going to show me something I couldn't get out of." He will reply, "Well, you can't, but I have to put my hands behind your head first." At that time simply reply, "If you can get me in it, I'll show you how to escape from it." This usually stops your friend, and you can go on about your business.

    Among the many ways to escape from this technique, one of my favorites is shown in Figure 74. Once the attacker has you firmly secured, use the outside edge of your left or right foot (for our purposes, use the right foot) and scrape the front of his right shin all the way from just below his knee to the top of his foot. Then, using your heel, stomp with vigor on the top of his opposite foot (in this case his left). As the attacker sways from right to left, direct your force down with your right elbow to break his hold on your neck.

    Now, quickly raise your left hand straight up as if reaching for something directly above your head (Figure 75). Simultaneously, take your right hand and pinch the attacker's testicles. (Pinching one will do.) If the attacker is wearing tight pants and the testicle pinch is not possible, use the back of your fingers to strike his groin. (In case you are a female and are unaware of the fact, this area of a man is highly sensitive.) The attacker's kuzushi will first be right forward with the stomp, then left forward with the heel strike, and then straight forward with the groin attack. The technique will conclude with off-balancing him straight back. Getting back to the technique, you will now position your feet in front of the attacker's feet on lines 7 and 8, toes pointing forward and to the outside. (Some people in karate call this stance a *kiba dachi* or *fudo dachi*.) Then slide both hands down the attacker's backside coming to rest just behind his knee (Figure 76).

    [*Note:* The kiba dachi can best be explained as follows: Plant the heels firmly on the ground, with the toes pointing straight forward. The feet are about double-shoulder

Figure 75

Figure 76

Figure 77

Figure 78

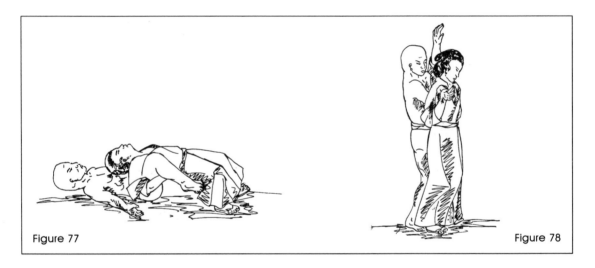

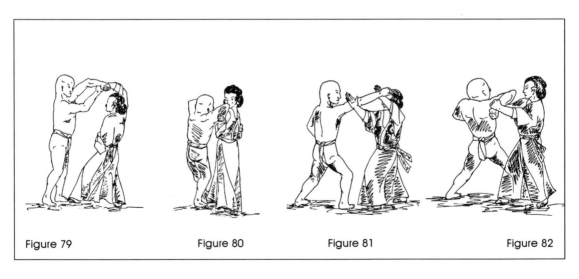

Figure 79

Figure 80

Figure 81

Figure 82

width apart; both knees are bent slightly outward. Your weight is distributed evenly on both legs. Keeping your knees directly over your big toes, tighten your hip and leg muscles and keep your back straight. Remember, if your legs are too close together, your body will be too high. The center of gravity must be low so that your kuzushi is stable.]

If you are in the proper position and stance, your head will be in line with the attacker's solar plexus. The technique comes to life at this point. Strike the back of the attacker's knees or press in severely with the top of your thumbs while you strike with the back of your head to the attacker's xiphoid process (located in the same area as the solar plexus). Now, as shown in Figure 77, push back with your leg muscles and hips. The attacker will fall back. As he hits the floor, keep lifting up with his knees and strike again with the back of your head by arching your back as in an acrobatic back bend. Please review Figure 77 closely. This action completes the technique.

Perhaps, however, he is one of those diehards who refuses to give up, or perhaps someone gets you in a full nelson by surprise. However it happens, you want to escape. The simplest method of escaping from a full nelson is to take hold of the attacker's fingers. Any finger will do. I suggest one of the little fingers from the top hand. If the attacker has his fingers interlocked, then seize the middle finger. Simply pull backward on the finger and break it. If he hasn't released you, break the next finger, and the next, and so on. You have, in most cases, a total of eight fingers to choose from, excluding the thumbs (see Figure 78). If you have broken all of the attacker's fingers and thumbs and he is still holding on, however, I regret to inform you that you're in a lot of trouble, and there is nothing I can do to help you out!

Figure 78 is another escape from a full nelson. Simply reach up and grab the attackers fingers with your right hand. Twist downward and clockwise.

TECHNIQUE NUMBER 7: Four-Corner Throw (*Shiho Nage*)

This technique starts with tori's back to the front of the happo-no-kuzushi chart; uke is facing him. Uke reaches across with his right hand and seizes tori's right wrist, palm down. Our action begins in Figure 79 as uke attempts to strike with his left hand to tori's face. Tori steps with his left foot across his own body to line 8 while lifting his right hand upward to block uke's attack.

In Figure 80, tori now takes hold of uke's right wrist with his right hand. (You can use your left hand to assist in this motion by pushing in on the back side of uke's right elbow. This will take uke off-balance toward line 7.) Tori pivots 180 degrees clockwise on the balls of both feet. Keep your knees bent. Uke's and tori's right hands will pass over tori's head. Tori will be facing between lines 1 and 2. Uke should be thrown in the direction of line 2.

A variation of this technique starts with Figure 81. As uke reaches out to strike or push tori with his right hand, tori blocks the inside of uke's wrist with his left palm and steps forward toward line 5 with his left foot while reaching under and behind uke's right elbow with his right hand.

In Figure 82, tori then steps with his right foot along, but slightly behind, uke's right leg, pulls down on the top of uke's right elbow with the back of his right thumb and wrist, and pushes up and forward with his left hand. Uke's balance is broken backward. Tori then throws uke between lines 4 and 5. [*Note:* You can follow uke to the floor by keeping hold of his wrist and keeping pressure up with your forearm. Upon landing, pin the back of uke's right wrist to the floor and strike with your left hand to uke's throat.]

TECHNIQUE NUMBER 8: (*Kote Gaeshi*)

The waza shown in Figure 83 is familiar to all aikido students. Before this waza is practiced, both tori and uke must be satisfied that uke can execute proper ukemi. This is because, if the technique is properly executed, uke will be required to take a 270-degree fall (if tori does not release the wrist) or a 360-degree fall (if tori does release the wrist). In Figure 83, tori has his back to the front of the happo-no-kuzushi chart and uke is facing him. Uke grabs tori's left wrist with his left hand, while taking a small step forward with his left foot.

In Figure 84, uke now strikes with his right hand to tori's face, while sliding his left foot straight forward. Tori steps forward with his left foot, raises his left hand with palm toward uke's face, and blocks the attack with his left forearm by bending his elbow slightly. [*Note:* If the technique is done properly, uke will lose his grip on tori's wrist as shown in Figure 84.]

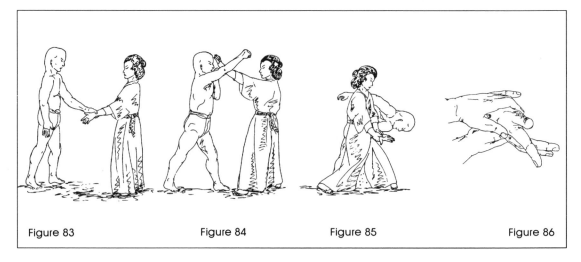

Figure 83   Figure 84   Figure 85   Figure 86

In Figure 85, tori immediately reaches with his right hand and places his thumb on the back side of uke's left hand while taking a firm grip with his fingers on the palm of uke's left hand. At this point, tori pivots clockwise on his forward foot so that his toes are pointing toward line 7 and steps around and behind with his right foot between lines 4 and 5, keeping the knee bent. He assists his left hand with his right hand by placing both thumbs on the back of uke's hand, forming a "V" with the thumbs. He pushes down, forcing uke to fall toward line 1.

Figure 86 is a close-up of tori's hand position. The novice must be extremely careful not to break his partner's wrist with this technique. It can happen very quickly.

Figures 87 and 88 show the same technique, *kote gaeshi*, but from a straight grab instead of a cross grab, as in the previous figures. Tori again has his back to the front of the happo-no-kuzushi chart. Uke grabs hold of tori's left wrist with his right hand. Tori turns his left wrist counterclockwise and brings the palm of his left hand in front of his face while stepping with his right foot to line 6. He reaches with his right hand and places his right thumb on the back of uke's right hand. He then pivots counterclockwise 180 degrees so that he is facing line 2. Assisting with his left hand, he throws uke in the direction of line 2.

Figure 89 is a close-up of the hand position that will take place between Figures 87 and 88.

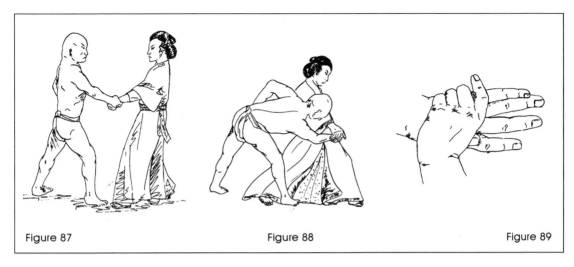

Figure 87   Figure 88   Figure 89

TECHNIQUE NUMBER 9

Figure 90 simply shows how to attack after you have apprehended someone's foot. Assume, as in the figure, that someone has kicked at you with his left foot. We are not speaking of a karate kick but, rather, a football type of kick that involves a long circular motion. As this happens, step to the inside, not trying to stop the foot on its way up but capturing the calf on its way down. (This is what has happened in Figure 90.) Now push

Figure 90   Figure 91

upward with your right arm, breaking uke's balance backward. With the ball of your left foot, kick as hard as possible into uke's right shin.

In Figure 91, you have completed the above motions. [*Note:* Here the attacking kick is with the right foot.] Simply pull forward on uke's ankle, take hold of uke's left shoulder with your right hand, balance yourself on your left foot, and step behind uke's left leg with your right leg. You can also sweep with your right leg, but this will cause uke to take a tremendous back fall; *be careful.*

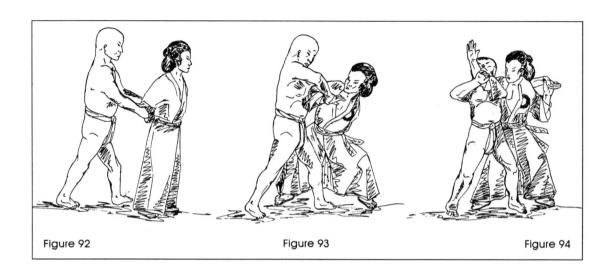

Figure 92   Figure 93   Figure 94

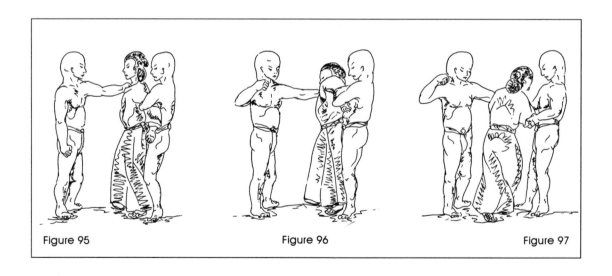

Figure 95   Figure 96   Figure 97

TECHNIQUE NUMBER 10: (*Ushiro Tekubi*)

We start this technique with uke and tori facing toward the front of the happo-no-kuzushi chart (Figure 92). Uke has seized tori's wrists from the rear and begins to push upward on them. (This is an excellent place to start your *fukushiki-kokyu*; this can be accomplished with a kiai that lasts the entire time it takes to complete this waza. When you are mentally prepared, let your total body relax.)

In Figure 93, tori steps with his right foot to his left rear, pivoting on his left foot. His left elbow will fold behind his back; he will be in a kiba dachi alongside uke as he places his right foot on the floor. Tori strikes uke in the solar plexus with his right elbow. The target area will be the xiphoid process. This is the lower third of the sternum.

In Figure 94, tori steps with his right foot behind uke's left leg, bringing uke's left arm, elbow pointing down, over his left shoulder. With uke's elbow on his left shoulder, tori pulls down with his left hand and, at the same time, strikes again with his right elbow to the uke's epiglottis. Tori now simply pushes down with his right arm. Uke will fall back over tori's right thigh.

[*Note:* The kuzushi for this waza will be forward, toward line 1 for Figure 92, back toward line 5 for Figure 93, and toward line 6 for Figure 94.]

We are going to conclude this chapter with two techniques involving situations where there are multiple attackers.

TECHNIQUE NUMBER 11

This technique begins with tori and uke No. 1 standing with their backs to the front of the happo-no-kuzushi chart (Figure 95). Uke No. 1 is holding tori from the rear, having grabbed under tori's arms just above his elbows. Uke No. 2 has seized tori from the front—in this case, with his left hand.

In Figure 96, uke No. 2 starts to strike with his right hand. Tori immediately straightens his left arm, enclosing the thumb into the palm of his hand and turns his left wrist clockwise until his elbow locks. Tori's fingers will be pointing toward the end of line 2. (It is important that, when you start this escape, you remove only your left arm from uke No. 1's grip.) Tori now steps slightly with his right foot to line 7 and, with a quick movement clockwise with his shoulders, leans slightly at the waist toward the ground and gives a quick jerk upward with his left arm.

Figure 97 shows tori's left arm released and his body pivoting clockwise on his right foot. Continuing in a circular motion to his right, tori keeps his right arm wrapped around uke No. 1's right arm and steps with his left foot around and in front of his right foot to line 8.

While this motion is taking place, tori strikes uke No. 1's right shoulder with the palm of his left hand (Figure 98). Uke No. 1's off-balance will be toward line 5.

Figure 99 reflects the beginning of the completion of this technique. Tori is now to the side, but slightly to the rear of, uke No. 1.

In Figure 100, keeping downward pressure on uke No. 1's elbow, tori directs him at uke No. 2, steps forward with his rear foot and slams uke No. 1 into uke No. 2. [*Note:* The distance between you and uke No. 2 will determine whether to push or throw uke No. 1. It is important to keep uke No. 1 between you and uke No. 2 at all times.]

Figure 98   Figure 99   Figure 100

TECHNIQUE NUMBER 12

It is hard for students to comprehend the technique shown in Figure 101, but I will attempt to walk you through it. In the figure, tori is facing to the front of the happo-no-kuzushi chart. Uke No. 1 is standing on line 3; uke No. 2 is standing on line 7. Each uke has hold of one of tori's forearms with both hands. Because two people are stronger than one, it is important to utilize the strength of one of the attackers against that of the others.

To accomplish this end, tori pulls down with his right hand, forcing uke No. 1 to pull toward himself with tori's right arm (Figure 102). At this point, tori and uke No. 1 are pulling against uke No. 2.

In Figure 103, tori lifts his right hand up and above his right shoulder, twisting his body slightly counterclockwise toward line 8. He steps with his left foot behind his right foot to line 2 and continues the overhead motion forward with his right hand. Tori should now be looking at uke No. 1's forearm. This movement should force uke No. 1 to pivot 180 degrees clockwise and allow tori to place uke No. 1's right forearm across the side of his face (Figure 104).

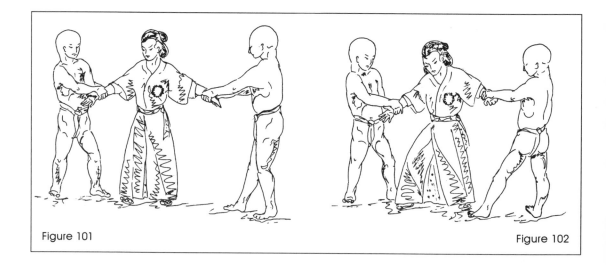

Figure 101   Figure 102

Figure 103

Figure 104

Keeping his forward motion going (Figure 105), tori places uke No. 1's forearm under uke No. 2's. In Figure 106, tori pushes down and to the rear of both ukes. He then slides with his left foot, and the technique is complete.

This concludes Chapter Three. We will now proceed to Chapter Four and *nage waza*, the art of throwing your opponent.

Figure 105

Figure 106

NOTES

1. Darrell M. Craig, *Iai, The Art of Drawing the Sword* (Boston and Tokyo: Charles E. Tuttle Co., Inc., 1981).
In this quote, the word *jujitsu* has replaced *iaido*.

> "Be as still as wood.
> Attack like the wind.
> Be as thorough as fire.
> Once we concur, be
> unmoveable as a mountain."
>
> —Takeda Shingen

CHAPTER FOUR
Nage Waza

IN THIS chapter we discuss ways to throw your opponent or project him away from you. It is most important to remember that *the hips determine the movement of both feet; the head determines the movement of both hands.* When you are throwing, you must never look at the uke after the throw starts; rather, look immediately to *where* you're going to throw. A good rule of thumb is that if you are throwing in a tight circle around your body, look directly at your little toe from the opposite side from which you are throwing. For instance, if you're throwing with a right-handed throw, look at your left little toe, and vice versa. Keep your opponent close to you and make your movements smooth and tight.

TECHNIQUE NUMBER 1: (*Obi Otoshi*)

This waza starts with tori's back to the front of the happo-no-kuzushi chart and striding line 1 (Figure 107). Tori is facing uke, who is striding line 5. Uke seizes tori in a front bear hug with his arms under tori's arms.

Figure 107   Figure 108

61

Figure 109

Figure 110

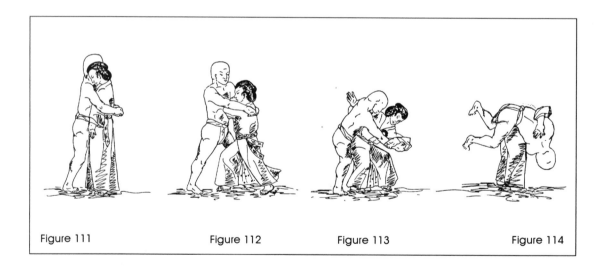

Figure 111

Figure 112

Figure 113

Figure 114

In Figure 108, tori reaches with his left hand and pinches severely under uke's right armpit. He could also fake a right knee to uke's groin. Either one of these movements will start uke's forward movement. As uke leans forward, tori places his right foot between uke's legs toward line 5, reaches with his right hand over uke's head, and takes hold of the back of uke's trousers or belt. Tori's right armpit should be resting on the right side of uke's neck.

In Figure 109, tori now falls backward by pulling toward line 1 and pushing straight down on the back of uke's neck with his right hand, grabbing the hollow of uke's armpit with his left hand and throwing.

Figure 110 shows the conclusion of obi otoshi. While tori's right hand is secured on uke's belt, tori slides his body quickly around toward line 6. This can be a rolling motion or half rolling motion, clockwise. Tori places the palm of his left hand on uke's right temple. With a push/pull motion—that is, pulling with his right hand and pushing with his left hand—tori is able to dislocate uke's neck.

TECHNIQUE NUMBER 2: (*Osae-Komi Uki-Goshi*)

In this waza, as in the previous, uke and tori are facing each other (Figure 111). Uke has his arms over and around tori's body. To have a secure hold, uke will probably have his right or left foot slightly forward. (The foot that is forward will determine whether you attack right or left.) Figure 111 shows uke with his left foot slightly forward; therefore, we will start the technique with our left hand. With his left hand, tori reaches between uke's legs and pinches uke's inner thigh or testicles. This will force uke to step back slightly with his right leg.

As shown in Figure 112, tori immediately steps forward and between uke's legs with his right foot, bringing his hands to his solar plexus with his elbows parallel with the floor. Using his forearms, tori pushes uke against uke's chest, forcing uke off balance backward toward line 5. [*Note:* Your pinch should create enough space between you and uke to allow your hands to move upward. If not, pinch harder.]

In Figure 113, tori pivots 180 degrees on his right foot while simultaneously placing his right arm under uke's left armpit. (Allow your left foot to follow your right foot during the pivot; your feet should be approximately 8 to 10 inches apart. Both knees should be bent so they are directly over your big toes.) Tori slides his left hand down and secures uke's right wrist. He then starts turning his head and looks at his left little toe.

Figure 114 shows the simple conclusion of this throw. Tori continues pulling uke's right arm with his left hand in a circular motion toward tori's left knee. With his right hand on uke's back, tori points his right index finger in a downward circle while leaning forward slightly toward his left little toe. Both uke and tori, just before the execution of the throw, will be facing the front of the chart. At the conclusion, uke will land on his back, feet toward line 3 and head toward line 7.

TECHNIQUE NUMBER 3: (*Ashi Nage Otoshi*)

This waza is entirely worked on migi-maesumi-no-kuzushi. I am purposely leaving out the line number because by now you should have mastered the chart. If not, please restudy the chart before proceeding to ensure that you understand which line we are working.

Figure 115

Figure 116

Tori again is striding line 1 with his back to the front of the happo-no-kuzushi chart. In Figure 115, uke steps forward with his right foot and punches at tori's face with his right fist. Tori steps forward with his right foot and blocks uke's strike with his left forearm. Tori then immediately takes hold of uke's right wrist.

The moment he secures uke's wrist, tori places his left foot on top of uke's right instep (Figure 116). Tori places his right hand behind uke's neck and pulls toward migi-maesumi-no-kuzushi with both hands. Tori slowly falls to the floor to his left; uke falls toward his right little toe on migi-maesumi-no-kuzushi.

Figure 117 shows the conclusion. Uke should try to do a forward somersault and land on his left side. For him to do so, tori must release his right hand from uke's neck so tori maintains his left-handed grip.

Figure 117

TECHNIQUE NUMBER 4: (*Shuto Otoshi*)

This technique is self-explanatory. Uke strikes with his right hand, stepping forward with his right foot (Figure 118). Tori blocks with his left hand sliding forward slightly with his right foot.

Figure 118   Figure 119   Figure 120

As tori makes contact with his left forearm (Figure 119), he immediately strikes the left side of uke's neck with the edge of his right hand. Simultaneously, tori pivots on his right foot, bringing his left foot around and behind, counterclockwise to line 6. Tori goes down on his left knee as he does so.

As uke leans forward, tori takes hold of uke's attacking wrist with his left hand and pulls toward his waist. Placing his right hand slightly behind uke's neck, tori moves his right foot forward on line 3 about 12 inches. Tori's right knee is pointing toward line 8. Tori throws uke over his right knee in the direction of line 8. [*Note:* In Figure 120, we find a poorly executed technique resulting in a poor throw. Try to avoid looking like this! Figure 120A reflects the proper foot positions for this technique.]

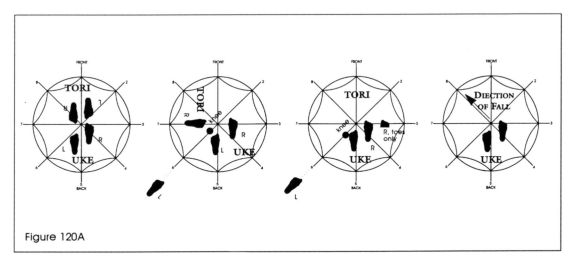

Figure 120A

TECHNIQUE NUMBER 5: (*Empi Seoi Nage*)

This waza will be relatively simple to most judo people. Again, I must stress kuzushi, tsukuri, and kake in that order. You must first off-balance your attacker; then and only then can you make your entry. Thereafter, the execution of the technique will be quite simple.

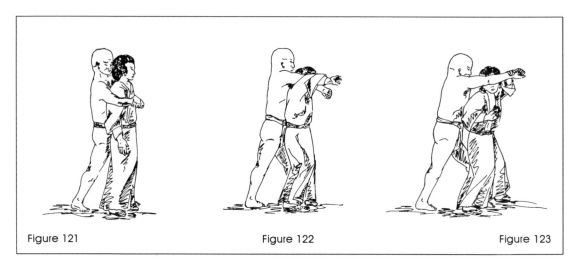

Figure 121   Figure 122   Figure 123

In Figure 121, uke has tori in a rear bear hug; uke's arms are around tori's biceps. When I teach this technique at the police academy or to police officers, I immediately get the "what if" question. Instead of waiting to listen to what I have to say, somebody interrupts and says, "Well, what if he doesn't grab you around the biceps, but grabs you lower around the elbows?" My reply is usually the same, "Well, come here and show me." Of course, the person is usually reluctant to do so, but with a little bit of encouragement and a lot of ego on his part, he usually complies with the request. I am about 5 feet 8 inches tall; usually, the person with the question is 6 feet or more. Regardless of his height, the attacker has to squat to bear hug me from the rear around my elbows. Usually, he wants to show his superiority, and how strong and manly he is. Of course, this attitude works to my advantage. Goliath seizes David from behind, squatting low as he does so. Very calmly, David simply brings the heel of his right or left foot sharply into the testicles that are hanging so low and vulnerable. The heel kick is simple: it's just like kicking yourself in the buttocks with your own heel. If you can convince your uke to try this maneuver, you'll find it works. With the "what if" question disposed of, let's get back to empi seoi nage.

In Figure 122, tori bends his knees over his big toes while forcing his elbows up,

Figure 124   Figure 125

taking a small step backward with his right foot as he does so. This will break uke's balance to his rear on line 5. Immediately, tori takes hold of uke's right wrist with his left hand. Tori then pulls toward line 2 pivoting slightly on both feet as he does so. His body will now be facing slightly between lines 1 and 2.

In Figure 123, tori strikes with his right elbow to uke's right rib cage. As uke leans forward from the elbow blow, tori steps back with his left foot and aligns his feet approximately 6 to 8 inches apart (Figure 124). He places his right bicep under uke's right arm.

In Figure 125, tori bends his knees over his big toes and throws uke over his right side. If the throw is executed properly, uke should land in the vicinity of line 1, with his head pointing toward tori's left foot.

TECHNIQUE NUMBER 6: (*Yoko Seoi Tomoe*)

This technique also starts with tori striding line 1 (Figure 126), facing the center of the happo-no-kuzushi chart. Uke steps forward with his left foot and strikes with his left hand to tori's face. (This situation could also involve someone reaching with his left hand to grab you and punch you with his right hand. However the technique starts, the conclusion is the same.) As uke strikes, tori steps forward with his right foot and blocks with his open left hand.

In Figure 127, tori immediately grabs uke's left wrist and strikes uke's left elbow with his right forearm. This will off-balance uke and cause him to step with his left foot across and in the direction of line 2.

Tori now finds himself slightly to the left side and behind uke. In Figure 128, tori places his right arm over uke's left arm and steps to line 2 with his right foot; only uke's right heel will touch the floor. This flowing movement resembles someone slipping on ice. Uke will counterbalance tori on their way to the floor. Both uke and tori are now descending toward line 2. [*Note:* To break uke's left elbow, tori would place uke's elbow rather than uke's shoulder under his armpit. Tori would then descend straight down and land on his buttocks. This is *very* dangerous for uke, be careful!]

Figure 129 shows the conclusion. Tori has pinned uke on his face and can twist the elbow or wrist joint to create pain or dislocation. Tori can use his feet and upper back as a tripod to control uke's movements.

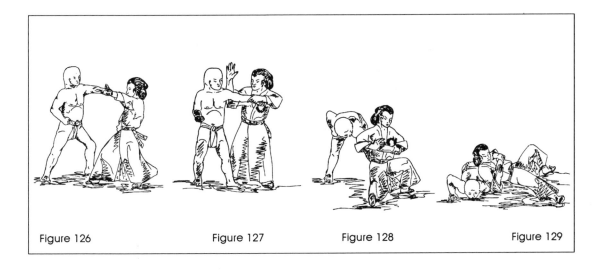

Figure 126   Figure 127   Figure 128   Figure 129

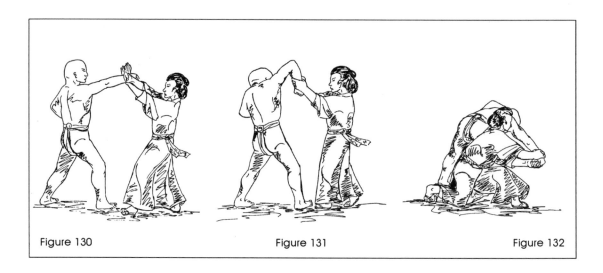

Figure 130   Figure 131   Figure 132

Figure 133   Figure 134   Figure 135

Figure 136   Figure 137

TECHNIQUE NUMBER 7: (*Kote Maki*)

This waza starts in the same fashion as the previous technique (Figure 130). Uke steps forward with his right foot slightly to the right side of line 5 and attacks with a grab or punch with his right hand to tori's face. Tori steps forward with his left foot just to the outside of uke's right foot and makes an X block upward at uke's right wrist. (Remember that tori's right hand is over his left.)

Upon making contact with uke's wrist, tori makes a circular motion to his right until uke's arm is about level with his shoulder. Tori grips uke's wrist with his right hand, and pulls slightly toward line 8. This will off-balance uke and cause him to step with his right foot in the direction of line 8. Tori continues the circular motion until he has come to the center of his body. In Figure 131, he then takes hold of the palm, just below uke's wrist, with his left hand. Upon securing uke's right forearm, tori pushes straight upward until uke's elbow is at a 90-degree angle.

Tori continues pressing upward on uke's wrist until it is just above tori's head. He then steps with his right foot 45 degrees to his left on line 4 and pivots 180 degrees to his left, allowing uke's wrist to rotate in his right hand in a natural motion while maintaining a firm grip with his left hand. (Be sure to maintain uke's balance off his left little toe toward line 8.) In Figure 132, tori uses his hands to throw by taking a small step forward with his left foot and simultaneously going down on his right knee. As he does so, he pulls uke's arm forward and downward in a circular motion until tori's hands come to rest in front of his groin. Uke will land on his back after completing a somersault on line 8. [*Note:* It is important to maintain a small amount of pressure in the direction of line 8 at all times.]

TECHNIQUE NUMBER 8: (*Kuzure Kani Basami*)

This technique, also known as the "modified scissors attack," is very similar to how a crab fights: by keeping its balance on one side of its body and catching its enemy with its legs in a scissor grip. A good chance to apply kuzure kani basami is when the attacker grabs you and moves his right leg forward to attack. This action will put you immediately in line with his right side and will make it easy to apply the moves described below.

The waza starts as did the previous technique. Again, uke steps forward with his right foot and attempts to strike or seize tori with his right hand. In Figure 133, tori responds by pulling uke's right hand with his right hand so that uke takes a step forward with his right foot. This move will make uke turn in a half-right direction.

In Figure 134, tori steps back and around with his right foot and places his left hand on the mat close to his left leg. Tori continues pulling with his right hand to keep uke's weight on his right side.

While using uke's weight for balance and supporting his upper-body weight with his left hand (Figure 135), tori hooks his left heel behind uke's right ankle. Simultaneously, tori brings his right foot up and smashes down on uke's right knee.

The action in Figure 135 will immediately throw uke backward. To avoid losing contact, tori quickly places his right leg behind uke's right knee and slides his left foot in front of uke's right ankle (Figure 136). (Keep a firm grip on uke's wrist with your right hand.)

In Figure 137, tori now quickly scissors uke's leg by pulling with his right leg and pushing with his left leg.

TECHNIQUE NUMBER 9: (*Yoko Ashi Gatame*)

Again, uke steps forward with his right foot and reaches for tori with his right hand. In Figure 138, tori takes his left hand, palm open, and pushes the side of uke's wrist clockwise (from 12 o'clock to 9 o'clock) while stepping back with his right leg. Tori twists uke's wrist so that his elbow is pointing straight up and quickly applies pressure with his right forearm on uke's elbow, thereby breaking uke's balance forward. Figure 138A shows the blocking used in the first motion.

As uke leans forward (Figure 139), tori quickly swings his right leg over uke's head, bringing his knee to his chest, and pushes his foot down between uke's legs. See also Figure 139A.

In Figures 140 and 141, tori grasps uke's waist with his right hand, and applies pressure with his right leg on uke's elbow. Tori then sits directly down on his left heel and pulls strongly forward with his right hand.

As uke completes his forward somersault (Figure 142), tori pulls quickly with his left hand, keeping uke's shoulder between tori's legs. Uke's elbow will now be pointing directly down into tori's lower abdomen.

In Figure 143, tori places his left leg over uke's neck and his right leg over uke's chest. Tori pushes down with his knees, taking hold of uke's wrist with both hands, and pushes up with his hips to break the elbow.

TECHNIQUE NUMBER 10: (*Yoko Te Gatame*)

In this technique, the first motion of the attack and defense is described exactly in Figures 138 and 138A above. In Figure 144, we pick up the action as uke loses his balance and leans forward toward the front of the happo-no-kuzushi chart. Tori continues sliding his right hand down between uke's legs and takes hold of the back of uke's right thigh. This is accomplished by stepping with his right leg between and beyond the back of uke, allowing his left leg to follow. (Keep pressure against uke's elbow in a downward motion with your right arm.)

In Figure 145, tori's feet slide forward so that he is almost sitting on uke's right foot. In Figure 146, tori lifts with his right hand and throws uke over his right shoulder. [*Note:* With the right hand action, tori is capable of applying a strike to the groin or squeezing the testicles.] Uke should land parallel to tori. As uke's head rises to complete his somersault after landing, tori applies a strike to the bridge of uke's nose with the back side of his left hand.

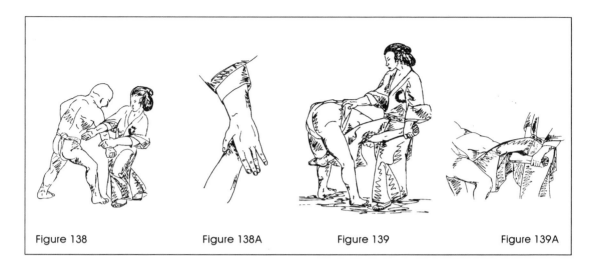

Figure 138   Figure 138A   Figure 139   Figure 139A

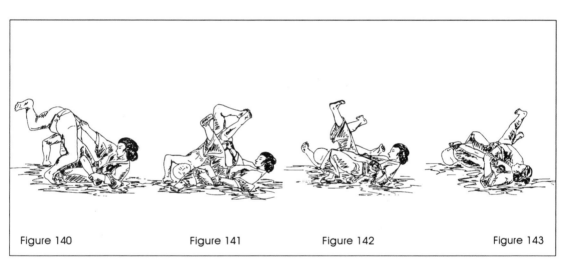

Figure 140   Figure 141   Figure 142   Figure 143

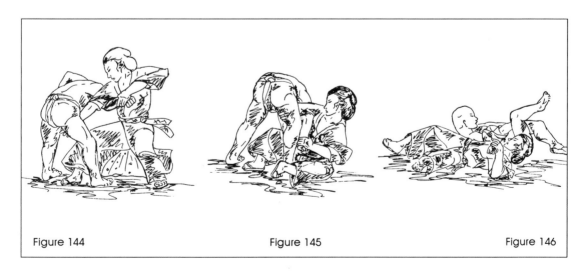

Figure 144   Figure 145   Figure 146

Figure 147

Figure 148

Figure 149

Figure 150

TECHNIQUE NUMBER 11: (*Kata-Guruma*)

Great care should be taken with the execution of this technique due to the violent nature of the throw. Again, the technique starts with uke stepping forward with his right foot and attempting to strike tori's face with his right hand. In Figure 147, tori steps forward with his right foot and blocks the blow with his left forearm. Immediately upon contact with his left forearm, tori twists his left hand counterclockwise, grasping uke's right wrist as he does so.

As uke steps forward on his right foot, tori pulls uke's right arm over the back of his neck and, as balance shifts forward to his right foot, steps deeply with his right foot between uke's legs. Tori keeps his legs apart for balance. With continuous pulling with his left hand, tori slides his right shoulder under uke until it touches uke's right hip. Tori immediately takes hold of uke's right thigh with his right forearm and hand (Figure 148).

In Figure 149, tori lifts uke straight up on his shoulders and executes the throw by standing upright, lifting uke's legs with his right hand, and pulling uke violently over his shoulders with his left hand.

Immediately upon landing (Figure 150), tori slides his left leg under uke's right arm and finishes by breaking the arm over his leg.

TECHNIQUE NUMBER 12: (*Empi Nage*)

This technique is quite similar to, and most likely the forerunner of *ippon seoi nage* (one-arm shoulder throw). As uke reaches out with his right hand either to grab or punch, tori steps immediately with his right foot across his body (Figure 151). He places his right arm under uke's attacking arm just above uke's elbow. Simultaneously, tori reaches with his left hand to uke's wrist and turns it so that the elbow is pointing down. Tori now moves his left foot back toward uke so that his feet make a "T."

In Figure 152, tori steps with his right foot just outside of uke's right foot, while placing uke's elbow on top of his right shoulder palm facing up. To execute this throw, tori simply sinks his hips, bends his knees and bends his body forward, turning his head to his left as he does so (Figure 153). [*Note:* Extreme caution should be taken in practicing this throw so as not to break or dislocate uke's elbow.]

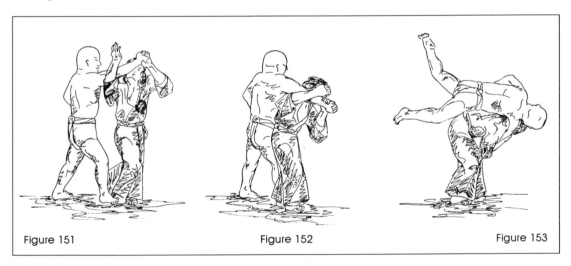

Figure 151   Figure 152   Figure 153

We dedicate the rest of the chapter solely for uke's rehabilitation. It is called *kappo*, the Japanese version of "how to keep your uke oiled and maintenance-free."

KAPPO: SYSTEM OF FIRST AID AND RESUSCITATION

I have found that many senseis know very little about kappo and little, if anything, about first aid. I believe that a sensei of a *montei* (pupil or disciple), whether a mudansha or yudansha, has a responsibility to know about such things.

In the old ryus, it was most important to tend to the montei if he was injured or rendered unconscious. Accordingly, in the early 1700s, kappo was developed by jujitsu masters. Since that time numerous senseis have added to and refined the art. Certainly, every teacher of a martial art need not be a doctor; moreover, it is not the sensei's responsibility to diagnose the extent of any injury. However, every sensei should have at least an awareness of the possible injuries that may be sustained in his class and the ability to provide minor first aid or preliminary care until the injured person can see a proper health care professional. All students' complaints, whether they concern shortness of breath, heat exhaustion, or muscle cramps, should be taken seriously. Only the student can really feel the pain. The following paragraphs detail the symptoms and treatment of some common injuries that could occur during a jujitsu session.

The following is not intended to be used as a medical guide. If you sustain any type of injury, please consult a physician for proper diagnosis and treatment.

INJURIES

Nose Bleed
Symptoms: Blood draining from the nasal passages. Possible pain in the nose area.

Treatment: Seat the person and tilt his head back. Apply finger pressure on his upper lip, cold wet towels to his nose, and a cold ice pack to the back of his neck. Then pack the nostril with a gauze roll. Do not allow the person to blow his nose. If bleeding continues or is profuse, see a physician immediately. [*Note:* Always treat a bleeding person with extreme care. Avoid coming into direct contact with someone else's blood.]

Broken Nose
Symptoms: Pain in the nose area. Nasal cartilage is torn away from the bone. Often severe bleeding.

Treatment: Gently move the injured area back and forth and feel for crepitation or a slight grating. To temporarily reset, which should be attempted ONLY if there is NO grating, place the thumbs on the sides of the nose using a slight downward pressure to relax and separate the cartilage away from the bone. Gently ease the cartilage back into position. Place gauze rolls on each side of the nose and hold them in place with tape. See a physician immediately as permanent nasal obstruction could occur if the nose is not correctly reset. The injured person should have an X-ray to ensure that the nose has been properly reset.

Dislocations
Symptoms: Bones that are normally in contact are torn apart and the related joint no longer functions. The joint may look misshapen and swollen. There is pain and skin discoloration. The joint may be immovable.

Treatment: Unless you are trained in the proper medical procedure, don't attempt to replace the disjointed joint. It is best to protect the dislocation and see a physician immediately.

Abdominal Injuries

Symptoms: pain in the abdominal area, such as soreness or cramping, accompanied by dizziness and nausea

Treatment: Treat individual injuries, depending on the extent of the pain. If pain is minor, rest and water may be needed. If pain is severe, the injured person may first need to be treated for shock before seeing a physician immediately.

Muscle Pulls

Symptoms: The muscle has been overstretched, causing the muscle fibers to be strained and possibly torn. There is pain when the injury occurs, and the muscle may be tender, swell, or become stiff.

Treatment: Apply ice to the area, as this will prevent swelling and decrease the pain. Aspirin may be taken to relieve the pain. Use the pulled muscle as little as possible for the next few days. For support, an elastic bandage may help.

Charley Horse

Symptoms: muscle spasm, accompanied by pain in the soft muscle tissue

Treatment: Kneel down in a catcher's position, or fold the leg under the body and sit on it. This action will prevent muscle contractions and/or hemorrhaging. With the knee in full flexion, wrap the area with an elastic bandage and ice packs.

Water on the Knee

Symptoms: A swelling or accumulation of joint fluid and blood around the knee joint, in front of and just below the kneecap

Treatment: Wrap the knee with an elastic bandage and limit physical activity until the knee returns to normal.

Sprains

Symptoms: pain, swelling, and possible discoloration of the skin

Treatment: Regardless of where the sprain occurs, it is a result of ligament tears at the joint. Accordingly, first wrap the joint with an elastic bandage. For the first twenty-four hours, putting an ice pack on the sprained joint may reduce swelling. Soak the sprained area in warm water and, if possible, keep it in an elevated position (this may help drain the fluid away from the swollen joint). After one or two days, try to exercise the joint, to prevent its stiffening.

Shock

Symptoms: A person in shock may sweat, appear pale, feel faint or drowsy, have cold moist skin and have a weak, but rapid pulse.

Treatment: As shock can follow any severe injury, first-aid treatment after all severe injuries should include measures to prevent or minimize shock. First, lay the conscious person on his back, face forward with feet raised. Then loosen any tight clothing and wrap him in a coat or blanket. Make the person as comfortable as possible until proper medical care can be received.

Resuscitation Techniques *(Kappo Ryu)*

During a practice session, especially after training in shime waza, a *judoka* may be choked into unconsciousness. The following two methods of resuscitation are the most commonly used. If, after applying the kappo ryu, the person does not begin breathing on his own or his breathing is irregular, immediately call for medical assistance and, until it arrives, treat the person for shock.

Inductive Method *(Sasoi Katsu)*
Sit the student up and fold one leg under the other leg's kneecap. Now, stand behind the student and place your knee in the middle of his back, lean forward and place your hands (fingers open) on the upper part of the chest, just below the shoulders. While pushing gently with your knee, press back with your hands until the student's back is straight, then let the body slowly lean forward until it is in a natural slump. Repeat this forward-backward motion at the rate of about ten to fifteen times per minute until the student regains normal breathing on his own.

Testicle Method *(Kogan Katsu)*
Kogan katsu is not really a method of resuscitation. Rather, it is a treatment for a man whose testicles have been kicked up into his pelvis. This injury could have been caused by a poorly executed kick or throw, such as *ouchi-gari* or *uchi mata.*

Sit the student in a cross legged position. Place your hands under his armpits from behind, lift him up gently and then let him drop down. Continue this procedure until the testicles have returned to their normal position.

THE IMPORTANCE OF WATER

The importance of drinking enough pure water and the relationship of water to preventive medicine are not recent discoveries. In 1904 Irving Hancock published a book about physical training. In it he noted:

> *At a very early date the samurai discovered the value of drinking a very considerable quantity of cool, pure water in every twenty-four hours. The amount consumed today by the average disciple of jiu-jitsu will reach the gallon mark.... Summer drinks, composed of shaved ice covered with fruit syrups, have crept into the life of the larger Japanese cities, but their use is not extensive, and the student of a jiu-jitsu school will have none of them. He is better taught.... From times of great antiquity, the athletic samurai understood the benefit of drinking only the purest of water.... The Japanese student of jiu-jitsu, when he finds a slight illness coming on, does not go to the doctor. The author is in the habit of drinking, normally, a gallon of water in twenty-four hours. Very recently he was threatened with tonsilitis. By practically abstaining from food, and by adding a half-gallon of water a day to the usual quantity, he prevented the threatened illness without regard to any medicines. And this treatment was begun after the throat became sightly ulcerated.... It is believed by the Japanese that complete health cannot exist unless the internal system is most effectively cleansed by the imbibing of very frequent draughts of water—cool, not ice cold. The intestinal tract is likened, by our clever little neighbors of the Orient, to the sewer, that requires vigorous flushing.[1]*

Most people do not have the slightest idea how much pure water—not meaning tea, coffee, lemonade, and such—they consume each day. Here is how to find out how little pure water you do drink. Set a quart jar, like a juice jar, by the kitchen sink. Every time you have a drink of water, take the same amount and pour it into the jar. Your consumption per day will probably be less than a quart. So my advice to you is: fill up those jars!

NOTES

1. H. Irving Hancock, *Jiu-Jitsu Combat and Tricks* (New York: G.P. Putnam's & Sons, 1904).

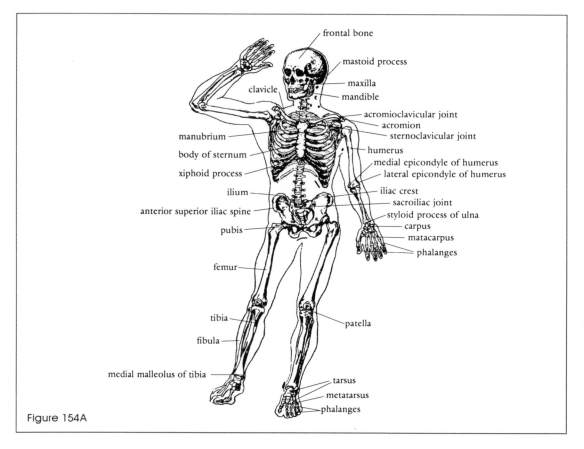

Figure 154A

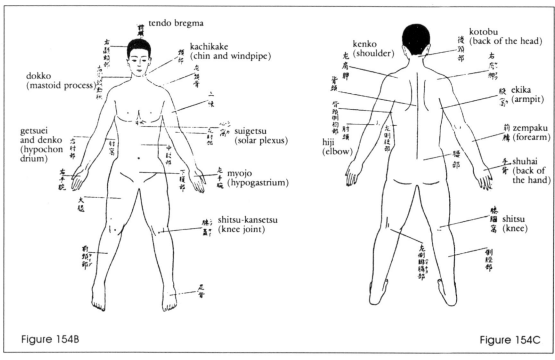

Figure 154B

Figure 154C

> **"**The Martial Arts is a lifetime study.
> It is not a matter of months or years,
> It is for life.**"**
>
> —Takahara Shinun Sho

CHAPTER FIVE
Atemi Waza

IN THIS CHAPTER we discuss *atemi waza* (or *ate waza*): how to locate pressure points, main arteries, and nerve centers, and how to strike and kick these areas with serious results.

Knowing where main arteries and nerve centers are located is one thing; finding and attacking them quickly on a resisting attacker is most certainly another. Mastering their location is a must for anyone wanting to learn the ancient art of jujitsu. To do so, it is imperative that you familiarize yourself with Figures 154A, B, and C. Figure 154A reflects the basic bone structure of the human body; whenever two bones articulate to make a joint, a good target is presented. Figures 154B and C are diagrams, provided by Sensei Hata, showing some of the more vital nerves and arteries. The purpose of this chapter is to show what areas of the body to attack and what part of your own body to attack them with. But first I want to address several interrelated topics: training by one-self, *ki, kiai,* and how to develop them.

TRAINING AND KI

I find it hard to always train with a partner. Of course, if you want to do your *awase waza, kyaku, or kansetsu waza,* you have to have an uke. But when you're alone and want to train, there are many options for you. I find that a useful tool to train in atemi waza is a *makawari,* which you can easily make with eight pieces of wood and a piece of cowhide. Go to a hobby shop that deals in hand-made crafts and purchase a piece of cowhide approximately five to six feet long and four feet wide. (It should cost in the range of $50 to $75.) It normally comes rolled up and thus is almost impossible to roll out flat; besides, it's as hard as a rock. Place the hide in a tub or large garbage can of luke warm water and allow it to soak until it becomes completely soft. Then remove it from the water and stretch it out to produce a piece that is approximately 62 inches by 50 inches. The extra 2 inches on each side are important for securing the hide to its frame. Return the hide to the water. Now you need to build a frame for the hide; 2x2-inch oak works well. You'll need four long pieces for the sides and four short pieces for the top and bottom. Angle irons can be used for the corners. Sandwich the hide between the two frames and secure it. It is important that you start securing at the top or bottom, not at the sides. If, for example, you secure the hide initially at the top of the frame, have someone help you slowly pull the hide tight as you work yourself down the frame. Secure the hide with screws approximately every 3 to 6 inches. Stretch the hide so that, when it dries, it will be as tight as a bass drum skin. The hide must be completely soaked while attaching it to the frame. The hide will have a tendency to dry quickly, so it's a good idea to lay wet towels on both sides while working.

Once you have built this contraption, let it dry until the hide is as hard as a rock. Then draw the torso of a man's front view on one side and his rear view on the other. Make the drawings as life-size as possible. If the hide is not large enough for a full-size person, just draw the area between the knees and the top of the head. Then mark on the hide the vulnerable areas reflected on Figures 154B and C. Make sure you check each area twice for accuracy. Drill a hole at each area; do not cut the holes with a knife. The hole size should not exceed that of your index finger. It is better to first drill a small hole, then use a metal eyelet around each hole. This keeps the hide from tearing and makes the target last longer.

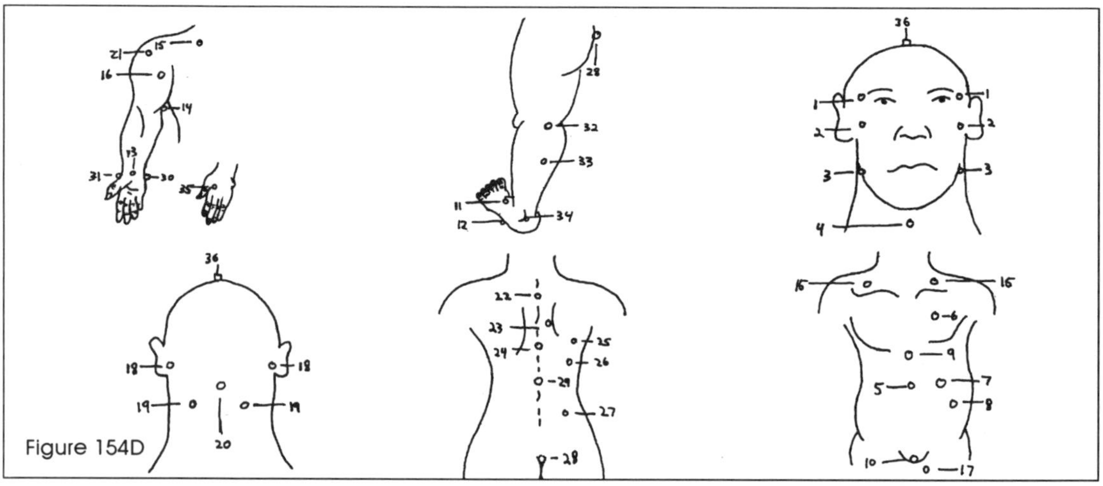

Figure 154D

Now that your target is complete, you can start practicing your atemi waza. First, you must memorize each vital area as reflected on the chart. You will learn through practice which part of your body to use on each area (see Figure 154D) and which of your weapons delivers the maximum power. When I first started training in atemi waza, I found it desirable to turn out the lights and, through only touch, locate each eyelet and name it. When you can locate several points efficiently, turn the lights on and turn your back to the target. Without concentrating too much, turn and attack a specific vital area. I used to think it was exciting to set a timer for two or three seconds and then relax; the instant the timer sounded I turned and attacked one of the areas. This is called *debana;* it means to move on movement—in this case, to move on sound. Keep in mind that this type of training does not develop strength as much as it does concentration of power to a small area. This type of training is essential for timing, balance, posture, coordination, and speed. But certainly, accuracy in finding a nerve or artery is essential.

Two other common methods of training by yourself using your hands are:

1. Paper training: simply crumple up a newspaper, place it on the table or the floor, and use the palm of your hands to spread it flat again as quickly as possible.

2. Candle training: light a candle and strike to extinguish it with a finger or part of any weapon shown in Figure 154E.

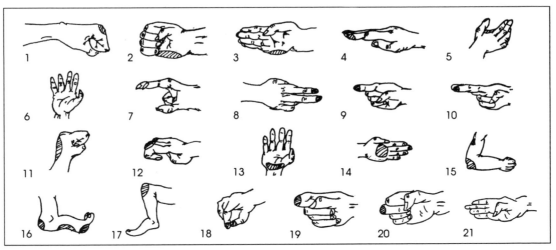

Figure 154E

Eventually, through your daily practice of kick, stab, jab, poke, and gouge, your reflexes will become automatic and your subconscious mind will take over. As I said in my book, *Iai, The Art of Drawing the Sword*, life is a road which starts without your consent at birth and ends without your consent at death. What you make of it between the beginning and the end is up to you. If you control your destiny and leave a mark on the minds of those who follow, you have done well; but if you leave nothing, you are but a leaf falling.

SHITAHARA AND *KIAI*

No martial art, old or new, would be complete without the *kiai*. We all know about the famous kiai. Almost every day we hear it in the movies and on television. Many people try to kiai with their throat muscles; but just making noise with your mouth is not a kiai. The true kiai comes from deep in the lower abdomen (we call it *shitahara* or *saika-tanden*) and is developed only through *fukushiki-kokyu* (deep abdominal breathing). Around the turn of this century, while living in Japan and studying judo under some great masters, E. J. Harrison wrote that "the word *kiai* is a compound of *Ki* (meaning mind, will, turn of mind, spirit, etc.) and *Ai* (the contraction of the verb *awaso*, signifying to unite). As this combination actually suggests, it denotes a condition in which two minds are united into one in such a manner that the stronger controls the weaker."[1] I have noticed in Japan that the best kiai is usually heard in a kendo hall or dojo. I suspect this is because, in kendo, you always call out in advance the area you are going to cut, thereby letting the other kendoist know exactly your intentions. Therefore, you are always taking air deep into your lower abdomen, which is, of course, the proper method for developing one's kiai.

Sensei Hata has told several interesting stories about old masters who accomplished almost unbelievable feats with their kiai. One story worth mentioning is about a jujitsu sensei named Nakasinkiri. As the story goes, Nakasinkiri Sensei was coming home from his afternoon workout. As he passed by a new building under construction, a worker fell from a scaffold about thirty feet from the sensei. A crowd quickly gathered about the fallen man. Someone in the crowd noticed Nakasinkiri and, knowing he was a jujitsu master, hurried over to him and asked for his assistance. It was well known that the bujutsu masters were versed in medicine, since dealing with broken bones and head injuries was a common practice.

After the normal formalities, the sensei agreed to see if he could be of some assistance. Kneeling down, the sensei carefully ran his hands up and down the body of the injured man. Then he asked everyone to please step back and put their hands over their ears. Once this had been done, he picked up the man's head and cradled it in his hands. He then took two or three deep breaths and let out a kiai that seemed to shake the very ground. The man opened his eyes, jumped to his feet, and ran off down the street.

Now I know there may be doubts about the accuracy of this story but, who knows what man can do once he has the *chikara* (power)?

How does one go about developing this mysterious power we seem to know so little about? One jujitsu sensei suggests taking a wide piece of cotton cloth about 12 inches by 8 feet, folding it widthwise in half (that is, to a width of about 6 inches), and wrapping it around your stomach two or three times just below the floating ribs. Make sure you pull your stomach muscles in as much as possible. Now sit in *seiza* (a straight position) or *anza* (quiet), inhale air through your nose, and try to push the air deep down into your stomach. The Japanese call this area *shitahara*. Inhale and exhale slowly two or three hundred times each day until you can do a thousand or more repetitions. You must start out very slowly and build up. At first, you will become very light-headed, so be extremely careful. While practicing this breathing with your abdomen, keep your body relaxed. The end of your nose should be in line with your navel, your shoulders should be rounded and your back should be bent forward just slightly. Once you have developed your shitahara properly, start practicing your kiai. Remember, start slowly from down within your stomach, keeping relaxed when you start your kiai. Relax every muscle except your calves. When you can accomplish this, then relax every muscle except your calves and your forearms. Thereafter, take one part of your body at a time and keep it rigid while kiaing very soft and low.

Sensei Hata said that once you can control your body muscles and develop your kiai, your body will respond subconsciously to your kiai. Thus, your muscles will remain soft and flexible until the precise moment you call upon them; at that point they will become rigid but only for the short time they are needed.

ACUPUNCTURE AND ATEMI WAZA

We frequently hear about acupuncture today; some people believe in it and some do not. Whether one believes probably depends on whether one has had personal experience with it and, of course, whether it worked. I have talked to several people who have had successful acupuncture, and I once met a sensei who was also a professional acupuncturist. Regardless of the pros and cons of the practice, I feel there must be more to it than meets the eye. When it was first introduced openly to the western world, not much was said about it. Then, suddenly, the medical profession adopted codes governing it. It is my belief that it does work and that medical professionals wanted to assure it was being performed by qualified people.

At its core, acupuncture involves the application of a knowledge of vulnerable parts of the body for curative purposes. It is interesting to note that this same knowledge also has application to atemi waza. The art of atemi waza consists of the following movements:

1. *ashi ate:* foot strikes
2. *hiji ate:* elbow strikes
3. *hiza-gashira ate:* kneecap strikes
4. *kobushi ate:* fist strikes

To be successful in atemi waza (also known as the Kyusho method of jujitsu), one must first develop his fukushiki-kokyu, which we discussed previously. Fukushiki-kokyu is the key to atemi waza; it brings power to your feet and hands.

When I was in Japan training with Sensei Hata, he gave me a chart (Figures 154B and C) on vulnerable areas of the human body. According to this chart, which was 150 to two hundred years old, at certain times of the day or night certain parts of the human body are more susceptible to attack than at other times. It sounded very speculative to me. Later, as acupuncture became more widespread in the United States, I remembered that chart and began to study it. As I did, a whole new world opened up for me. I talked to several doctors concerning the chart's theory and, as usual, heard pros and cons. However, I did not find one doctor who said it was inaccurate.

If you practice jujitsu using this chart, you must use extreme caution: you may accidentally strike your mark and, unbeknownst to you at the time, cause serious or fatal injury to your partner. "His mind will lock his body in an ever lasting prison, from which there is no escape."[2]

Atemi Waza (or Ate Waza)
The Art of Attacking Vital Spots in the Body

12 A.M. to 2 A.M.	just above and centered on the top lip
2 A.M. to 4 A.M.	the bridge of the nose at eye level
4 A.M. to 6 A.M.	the top of the forehead, about where the hairline is
6 A.M. to 8 A.M.	in the hollow behind the jaw bone (by the ear lobe), about two fingers down
8 A.M. to 10 A.M.	the temple at eye level
10 A.M. to noon	about one inch above the nipples
Noon to 2 P.M.	the right or left wrist, where the pulse can be felt
2 P.M. to 4 P.M.	the middle of the chest or what we call the sternum to attack this area, you should use the end of your fingertips and push upward until you hit the backbone
4 P.M. to 6 P.M.	(Unavailable)
6 P.M. to 8 P.M.	the inner part of the thighs, about 8 to 10 inches down from the top
8 P.M. to 10 P.M.	behind the scrotum, between the testicles
10 P.M. to 12 P.M.	the soles of the feet, about 2 inches in front of the heel

Major Points of the Anatomy
(See Figure 154D)

1. Temple—*kasumi*
2. Side of ear—*kamumi*
3. Underneath jaw bone—*kachikake*
4. Adam's apple—*chikake*

5. Solar plexus—*suigetsu*
6. Above nipple—*myo*
7. Below nipple—(unavailable)
8. Edge of rib cage—*getsuei*
9. Sternum—*suigetsu*
10. Scrotum—*tsurigane*
11. Instep—metatarsus
12. Bottom of sole—*ashiura*
13. Inside wrist—carpus
14. Crazy bone area—*shitus*
15. Shoulder well—sternoclavicular-joint
16. Middle of bicep—humerus
17. Inner thigh—*kansetsu*
18. Behind ears—*dokko*
19. Underneath mastoid process—*dokksumi*
20. Nape of neck—mastoid process
21. Alongside shoulder—acromioclavicular joint
22. Alongside second vertebra—manubrium
23. Alongside shoulder blade—acromion
24. Between fifth and sixth vertebra—(unavailable)
25. 3 inches below shoulder blade—*horu*
26. Above the hip—*getsuei*
27. Between second and third rib from waist—*denkosuei*
28. Coccyx (tailbone)—(unavailable)
29. Weakest spot of spine—anterior superior iliac spine
30. Side of wrist—*horyu*
31. Side of wrist—styloid process of ulna
32. Behind knee—*shitsu-kansetsu ushiro*
33. Base of calf—*gashizahira*
34. Side of ankle bone—tarsus
35. Between thumb and first finger—metacarpus
36. Crown of head—*tendo*

Body Weapons and Appropriate Attack Areas
(See Figure 154E)

1. Forefist *(seiken)*	abdomen, chest, face, and neck; effective in blocking kicks, thrusts, and strikes
2. Bottom fist *(tettsui)*	used in downward or sideways strikes against mainly soft areas
3. Knife hand *(shuto)*	striking around the head area, face, shoulder, and abdomen
4. Spear hand *(yonhon-nukite)*	hand is parallel, with palm toward floor; used for thrust to abdomen, kidneys, throat, and armpit
5. Tiger mouth *(koko, also referred to as toho)*	scissors thrust to the front and side of neck.

6. Bear hand *(kumade)* — nose, under nose, and solar plexus

7. Three-fingered spear hand *(sheehon-nukete)* — pressure points, carotid artery

8. Two-finger spear hand *(nihon-nukete)* — same as above

9. One-finger spear hand *(ippon-nukete)* — eyes, under nose, solar plexus, and throat

10. Siamese fingers *(keiko,* sometimes called "chicken beak") — same as No. 7 and No. 9

11. Inverted or backfist *(ura-ken)* — strikes to the head

12. Half fist or dragon's head *(ryuto-ken)* — most effective in strikes straight ahead or on a horizontal line

13. Palm heel *(shotei)* — chin, face, or abdomen; also excellent in blocking attacks

14. Back hand *(haishu)* — same as No. 11

15. Elbow *(empi* or *hiji)* — solar plexus, lungs, under the chin, and back of neck

16. Heel *(kakato)*; knife foot *(sokuto)*; ball of foot *(chusoku)*; instep *(haisoku)*; arch *(teisoku)* — shin, abdomen, groin, ribs, kidneys, arms, and legs; because of the strength in your legs, the foot is an easy weapon with which to deliver the final blow when your opponent is down.

17. Knee *(hiza)* — groin, abdomen, and thigh

18. Eagle beak or chicken beak (still referred to as *keiko)* — same as No. 7 and No. 9

19. Forefinger one-knuckle fist *(hitosashiyubi-ipponken)* — eyes, throat and 90 percent of all nerves and carotid arteries

20. Middle-finger, one-knuckle fist *(nakayubi-ipponken)* — same as above

21. Spear hand *(nukite),* with hand perpendicular to floor with thumb up — same as above

22. Shoulder *(kata)* — solar plexus and head

I cannot overemphasize the extreme danger hidden within the techniques demonstrated in this chapter. I was even reluctant to include them in this book, but this is real jujitsu before 1882. As an example, the first waza is an attack to the armpit. To give you an idea of what can happen if you do not use extreme caution, a successful attack will cause pain and swelling in the target's armpit. After approximately fifteen minutes, a hard lump will appear there. A little later the target will experience a bitter taste in his mouth and a dry throat. He will then become nauseated. The next day he will lose his appetite, have difficulty breathing, and experience a sharp pain running from his affected arm down his rib cage to his hips. He will begin to cough, and the pain in his side will move to his chest. At this point, he will begin to vomit something that resembles a potato broth soup. He then experiences an overall loss of strength. Needless to say, if he hasn't figured out by then that something is drastically wrong and hasn't consulted a physician, he will die!

Figure 155   Figure 156

TECHNIQUE NUMBER 1

In this waza, you use body weapons 4, 12, 10, 18, 19, 20, or 21 for the best results.

In Figure 155, uke attempts to attack tori's throat. Tori is standing with his back to the front of the happo-no-kuzushi chart. Tori's heels are on lines 7 and 3. As uke attacks, tori moves his right foot clockwise so that he is facing line 7.

In Figure 156, tori blocks uke's attacking hand with his left hand, palm up, on uke's elbow, while stepping directly forward on line 5 with his right foot. Tori attacks with the tips of his fingers under uke's armpit, while maintaining a slight forward pulling motion with his left hand.

Figures 157 and 158 show basically the same footwork but using a different type of block or different attack.

Figure 159 simply shows tori moving into uke's attack and striking just under uke's chin at the Adam's apple using the *seiken* (forefist). You could also use the *toho, nukite, or hiji.*

TECHNIQUE NUMBER 2

In this waza, we attack a nerve beneath the clavicle, approximately three fingers from the throat (see Figure 154A). The soft area between the throat and the collar bone is easy to

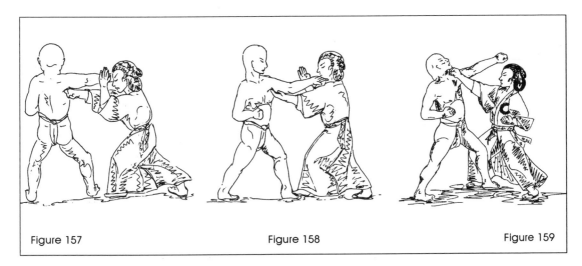

Figure 157   Figure 158   Figure 159

attack with body weapons 4, 6, 7, 8, 9, 10, 18, or 21. A strong attack in this area can pre-vent blood from circulating to the brain, causing death. Unfortunately, swelling will not appear until later, but the target's complexion will turn white and pale, and his feet and hands will become weak and have a rubbery feel. This is followed by headaches, ringing in the ears, cold sweat, and intermittent loss of consciousness. If these symptoms appear, the person must see a physician immediately. Without proper treatment, he could be in a very serious, if not deadly, condition.

I'm not going to get into the particulars of your feet in this waza. I think the draw-ings, explanation, and your prior hard work with the happo-no-kuzushi chart will lead you through these three figures. Nevertheless, if you have difficulty, I suggest that you return to Chapters 1 and 2. Do not place the cart in front of the horse!

Figure 160 shows tori blocking uke's attacking arm with his left hand. With his right hand, he makes a circular motion up and then down, striking the artery under uke's collarbone.

Instead of blocking to the outside, the technique shown in Figure 161 can be used if uke grabs your collar or pushes or strikes at you. Tori blocks with his left hand and attacks uke's artery using body weapons 4, 6, 7, 8, 9, 10, or 21.

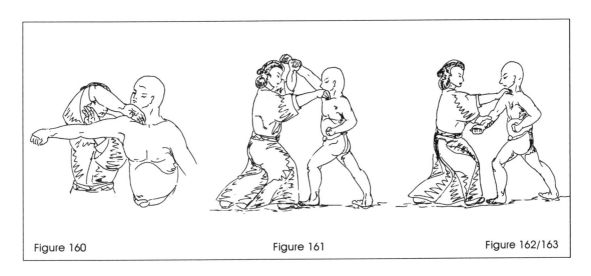

Figure 160   Figure 161   Figure 162/163

Figure 164

Figure 165

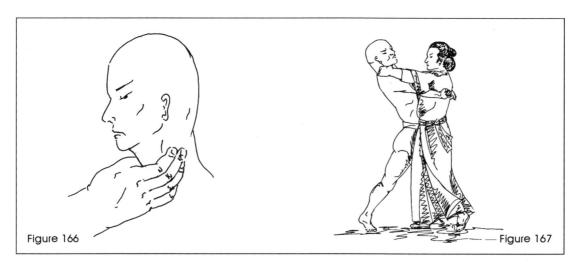

Figure 166

Figure 167

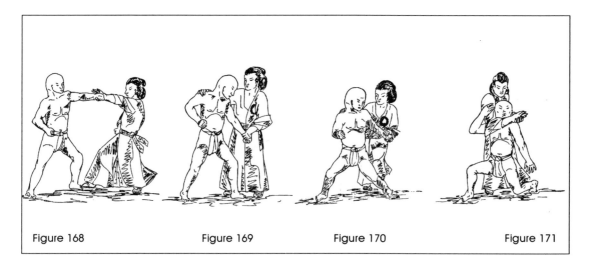

Figure 168

Figure 169

Figure 170

Figure 171

Figure 162/163 shows a very simple way of attacking this vital area. Tori simply grabs uke's right wrist with his left hand, turning counterclockwise so the palm is facing up and the elbow is down. Tori then attacks with body weapons 6 or 18. I prefer 6 because once I reach the depth of the well and uke is on his knees, I close my fist as I would to grasp a suitcase handle and break the collarbone. *Be extremely careful!*

TECHNIQUE NUMBER 3

In Figure 164, tori seizes uke's right wrist with his right hand and pulls toward line 1. In Figure 165, tori maintains a constant pulling motion with his right hand. He steps to uke's right side and strikes just under uke's neck using body weapons 2, 3, 14, or 21. Here tori has struck just below the ear, using the side of the hand. This can cause damage to the vertebral vein, jugular vein, carotid artery, laryngenial nerve, and thyroid cartilage. And, if the cervical vertebra is cracked or broken, it will result in massive hemorrhage and quick death.

By using the hand in a *koko* method (Figure 166), you will most likely fracture the thyroid bone or cricoid bone—needless to say, rupturing the jugular vein (to the brain), the carotid artery (to the brain), the vagus nerve, and the phrenic nerve. It will also rupture the trachea (windpipe). All of these injuries will cause blood leakage from torn blood vessels and, if the tear is not mended immediately, death by strangulation. A blood clot will form around the neck and grow larger with each beat of the heart. Eventually, this clot will press against the windpipe and nerves and will totally close them off. Any such fracture of the vertabra in this area is extremely dangerous. The least of the injuries will be similar to a whiplash. So *be careful* in your practice.

Figure 167 shows a very simple method of attacking this area. Here the suspect has tori around and under the arms in a bear hug. Tori simply steps forward with his right or left foot. Using his thumbs, tori jabs quickly to both sides of uke's Adam's apple. His thumbs should penetrate deeply enough to bruise the windpipe or trachea.

TECHNIQUE NUMBER 4: (*Kobushi Shime*)

This waza starts with tori's back to the front of the happo-no-kuzushi chart, bestriding line 1. Uke is facing tori and strikes out with his left hand. Tori immediately steps with his right foot to line 7 and blocks with his left hand (Figure 168).

In Figure 169, tori has taken hold of uke's left wrist and pulled slightly toward line 8. Aligning his left foot with his right and now facing toward line 3, tori simultaneously reaches behind uke with his right hand and places that hand on uke's right shoulder, continuing the kuzushi toward line 8.

In Figure 170, tori steps with his right foot behind uke. Tori is now facing to the front and line 1.

In Figure 171, as tori brings his left foot in line, he places it on the back of uke's knee and stomps downward while taking his right hand and forearm and sliding it under uke's chin. Tori now brings his right knee into uke's spine, forcing him backward. [*Note:* While replacing the attacking foot on the ground, it is important to control uke's body with your legs and feet from behind.]

For the best results in reaching the proper position for the *shime*, follow these steps carefully: from behind his right ear, slide your right hand leftward along the right side of his neck. Keep the back of your right hand in constant contact with his neck. Place the back of your left hand on his left shoulder, keep the inner edge of your right forearm on his neck, and clasp your hands together. Project your right shoulder forward by bringing the right side of your face close to the left side of his. Press his right carotid with the inner edge of your right forearm. Totally control uke's body movements from behind; if you don't, you are very likely to improperly apply the technique. Be sure to slide your hand under uke's chin from shoulder to shoulder; do not bring your forearm over and in front of uke's face; so doing will cause you to place your forearm on his jaw instead of under his chin. Be sure to keep close contact with uke's neck with the inner edge of your hand and forearm; this will prevent uke from placing his hands between your forearm and his neck to loosen your strangling pressure. You should also press your right shoulder joint toward the rear of uke's neck to assist your right forearm in giving the proper amount of pressure to uke's carotid.

It is important to know the difference between a choke and a strangulation. A choke is a controllable method of judo practitioners; it allows the technique to develop so that the recipient has the opportunity to "pat out." A strangulation, however, involves tying a person's hands behind his back, putting a rope around his neck, tying one end around a guard rail, and throwing him over. The object here is very clear: it is not meant to restrain or allow his surrender, but to cause death. This reminds me of a story I read several years ago. A mob captured a person who had raped a child. The mob tied his hands behind his back, put a rope around his neck, and threw him off the bayou bridge. Unfortunately for the suspect, the rope was longer than the distance to the ground, so when he hit the ground, the mob was angrier than ever. They pulled him up by the rope, retied it, and repeated the process. This time they accomplished their goal. And *that*, my friend, is truly a strangulation.

Unfortunately—or fortunately, depending on whose side you're on—a lot of law enforcement agencies have banned any type of restraining technique considered to be any type of choke, let alone something called a strangulation.

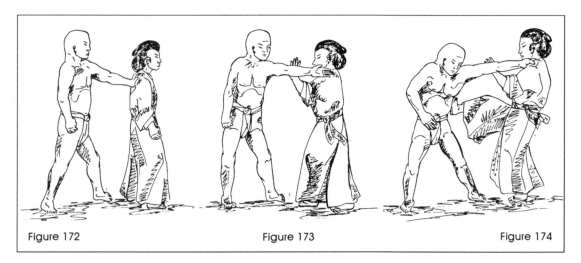

Figure 172   Figure 173   Figure 174

TECHNIQUE NUMBER 5: (*Hen-o-guruma shime*)

This technique begins with tori and uke facing the front of the happo-no-kuzushi chart. Tori is just in front of lines 3 and 7, and uke is actually standing on lines 3 and 7. In Figure 172, uke takes hold of tori's right shoulder with his left hand as if to pull him around clockwise and strike him in the face. (Some Texans refer to this as a "sucker punch.") As uke pulls on tori's shoulder, uke steps back with his right leg.

As tori feels uke's threatening move (Figure 173), he immediately moves counter-clockwise with his right foot to line 8, pivoting 180 degrees and blocking uke's left arm with his left hand.

In Figure 174, tori kicks uke's rib cage with his right foot. [*Note:* Two things can happen when attacking this area. One, if the attack is not done properly, you will only fracture but not break the continuity of the rib bone. This type of injury will cause only discomfort and pain while breathing. A proper—that is, severe—attack should result in a complete break of the bone. The broken ends will easily tear into the lungs, resulting in collapse of the lungs. If this occurs, death is but a short distance away. The danger, other than shortness of breath, with a completely collapsed lung is an uncontrollable spasm to the heart. Unknown to the layman, the heart is held in place primarily by the lungs. When there's no lung pressure to help hold the heart in place, the heart will shift its position—in this case, toward the collapsed lung. This shifting will result in a severe muscle spasm and, usually, death.]

Figure 175   Figure 176   Figure 177

Immediately after tori kicks, he pulls uke's left arm downward and toward line 2 (Figure 175). This will force uke to take a step with his left foot to line 1; uke will then be facing line 2. As this kuzushi is accomplished, tori steps behind uke, pulling uke's left hand backward and placing his right hand (palm down) on the side of uke's neck. Tori slowly slides his right hand across to uke's left shoulder.

In Figure 176, as tori continues sliding the back of his hand under uke's chin, tori kicks the back of uke's left knee with his right foot and pulls upward under uke's chin. In Figure 177, tori continues to take uke to the floor with pressure applied to the back of uke's knee. Using his left hand, tori turns uke's left wrist so that his elbow is pointed toward the ground. By maintaining severe pressure under uke's chin and pulling back-ward, tori can slide his left foot to the rear and left side, go down on his left knee, and break uke's elbow across his right knee.

Figure 178

Figure 179

Figure 180

Figure 181

Figure 182

TECHNIQUE NUMBER 6

This waza is relatively simple but—as with all things simple—it can become complicated. It starts with tori's back to the front of the happo-no-kuzushi chart and uke facing him. Uke steps forward with his right foot and seizes tori's left wrist with his right hand (Figure 178).

In Figure 179, tori raises the fingers of his left hand so that his palm is facing uke. Using pressure with the outside edge of his palm on uke's wrist, tori pulls uke toward line 2. This will off-balance uke toward line 2 with his right foot. Tori immediately strikes uke in the throat with his right hand, using the *toho* method. [*Note:* It is important to strike before uke completes his forward motion.] Tori simultaneously steps with his right foot behind uke's right leg toward line 4. This technique can be finished by forcing uke's body backward and over tori's right leg, a movement similar to osoto gari.

TECHNIQUE NUMBER 7: (*Yoko-tai-sabaki-keito*)

In describing this waza, I have a small surprise: *Waza hajime uke tai* tori's *hidari kote* with his *migi te* and proceeds to *zuki* with his *hidari te* or *mae geri keage* with his *hidari ashi*. (When uke grabs, do not pull away but look directly in his eyes, remembering that the eyes are the windows to his mind.) Now, when tori feels that uke is going to attack either by pulling or striking, he reacts by placing himself first in the *hidari shizen hontai;* that is, he stands with his *hidari ashi* and *te* advanced, as in Figure 180.

In Figure 181, tori, reacting with *debana*, pivots on his *hidari ashi* while opening his *hidari te* so the fingers and thumb are as far apart as possible. He pivots by moving his *migi ashi* behind his *hidari mae ashi* in a *maki* movement so that his *tai* will be beside uke. As he pivots, he extends his *hidari te mae*.

The movement shown in Figure 182 will break uke's kuzushi *mamae-no-kuzushi*. As uke starts to release tori's *kote*, tori raises uke's *ude* straight upward, pivots again on his *hidari ashi* counterclockwise, and steps behind uke's *migi ashi* with his *migi mata*. Then tori brings uke's *migi ude* in *mae* of tori's *tai*. Tori takes hold of uke's *migi te* with tori's *hidari te* and *harai* his *migi ashi* out from under uke. Tori then *atemi* uke's *hidari yoko kubi* with the *ouchi* of his *migi kote*. The kuzushi will now be *migi ushirosumi-no-kuzushi*.

[*Note:* The wrist strike (*keito uchi*) is an upward strike. You must use the full snapping motion of the wrist. With practice, you will find this technique to be a speedy one involving a minimum amount of motion.] The area you will strike will be the left carotid artery, just below the subject's earlobe. Don't forget to kiai. Regarding the sweep (*Osoto-otoshi*) see *Tenchi Nage*, Technique Number 1 in Chapter Three.

For those who would like to study in Japan, note that the above technique was taken directly from Hata Sensei's handwritten notes. It is not easy to decipher, but you can look the Japanese words up in the glossary. With some effort you may understand the technique just described. [*Note:* Claudia Smith and I translated most of the Japanese into English and also provided the line drawings. These drawings were not in Hata Sensei's notes, but were taken from mere stick figure drawings.] The point is that training in the great Nihon requires that you learn some Japanese.

TECHNIQUE NUMBER 8: (*Ten Ken-Kuzure*)

There are several modifications to the start of this technique, but the conclusion is always the same. As shown in Figure 183, uke grabs tori's clothing with his left hand. Tori first seizes uke's left hand with his left hand and turns uke's hand over one half turn counter-clockwise. Uke's thumb will be pointing toward the ground. Now, tori applies his right hand on top of his left.

In Figure 184, tori's little fingers will be on uke's wrist, pressing down on the pisi-form bone. As uke's kuzushi is broken downward, tori pushes backward with both hands and kicks uke in the groin area. (This technique is easy to apply if uke refuses to release his grip when tori turns his hand over.) Since tori has reached up and over uke's left wrist with his left hand and turned it counterclockwise, uke's thumb will be toward the ground. If uke releases his grip or tries in desperation to hang on, his thumb will be toward tori

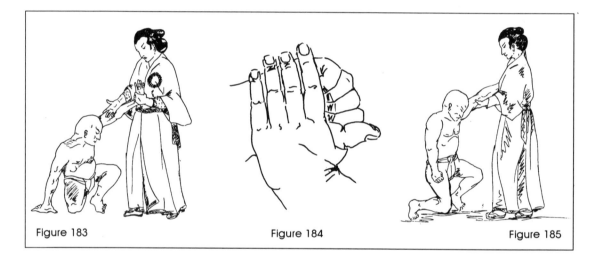

Figure 183   Figure 184   Figure 185

as in Figure 183. Tori now simply steps forward with his right foot, keeping downward pressure on uke's wrist, and breaks uke's balance backward. Using the edge of his right hand, tori applies pressure downward on the branchial plexus nerve located on the inside top of the uke's left elbow. This will break uke's kuzushi forward. As this happens, tori twists uke's left wrist counterclockwise with his left hand and steps behind uke's left arm, allowing him to slide freely to his stomach.

If you do not wish the subject to fall forward, but rather want him up on his feet, when he is in the position reflected in Figure 185, simply place your right hand under his left elbow, seize his ulnar nerve with your middle finger, and press straight upward. This will bring the subject straight upward on his feet. But be careful! The subject is now in a position to attack again. Thus, you must follow the subject's upward motion and, just before he achieves a standing position, push him backward or sideways so that he loses his balance and continues his journey to the ground.

Before we conclude this chapter, I would like to explain briefly how to make a drunk or a reluctant suspect stand up from a lying or squatting position. Located just under each of the suspect's earlobes and in line with his jaw bone you will find his facial nerve. It can be activated by pressing inward with your index finger. The best way to do this is to approach the suspect from his rear, place your index fingers on his facial nerves, press inward, then lift upward; the suspect will immediately rise to the occasion and stand at attention. In all my law enforcement teachings, I have never had an officer come back to me and say this technique wouldn't work. I must warn you again, however: your main purpose in law enforcement is to arrest, not to punish. At the same time, no one wants an officer to get hurt, so use all these techniques at your discretion.

NOTES

1. E. J. Harrison, *The Fighting Spirit of Japan* (Slough, England: W. Foulsham & Co.; distributed in the United States by Sterling Publishing Co.).
2. Peter Urban, *The Karate Dojo* (Boston and Tokyo: Charles E. Tuttle Co., Inc., 1975).

Top, left to right: Sensei Ichiro Hata, Sensei Setsuji Kobayashi, Darrell Craig.
Bottom, In 1979 at the Hokushinkan Chiba Dojo in Osaka, Japan, upon receiving the prestigious Haori samurai surcoats adopting the following students into the Chiba family: (*Left to right*) Patricia Metcalf, Mike Treyall, Darrell Craig, and Mary Ann Craig. Witnessed by Sensei Setsuji Kobayashi (Imperial Palace Police).

Top and bottom, A Japanese police envoy to the Houston Police Academy demonstrating kendo and judo.

Top and bottom, Osaka Police Department taiho jitsu class of 1975.

Top and bottom, Police academy cadets training in martial arts and the tea ceremony in 1975. I found the Japanese police academy quite different from our own; it reminded me of Marine Corps boot camp. The cadets were outstanding: polite, enthusiastic about their duties, and overwhelmingly courteous. Unlike our police academies, the Japanese have an unending list of college-degreed applicants for this prestigious duty.

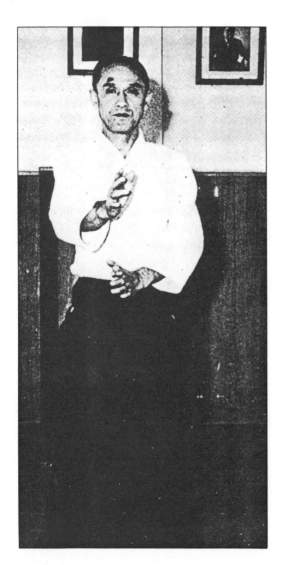

Left, Yoshinkan founder Sensei Gozo Shioda, 9th Dan.
Above, Sensei Shioda showing a waza similar to one in Chapter Three.

Right, top, Arato Kenshusea Funayama, yodan, showing the proper stance and an arm bar in Yoshinkan Aikido.

Right, bottom, Sensei Osaki Shigeharu from Tokyo, one of the top living swordsmiths. When I was president of the Houston Token Kai, I invited Sensei Shigeharu to Houston to give a lecture on the Japanese sword and to show his craft. He is truly an outstanding craftsman in an art that is slowly giving way to modern methods. Even though he has an electric hammer to pound the metal, he still prefers that an apprentice do it. But as in all traditional Japanese arts, he stated, "It is almost impossible to find a suitable apprentice who understands the labor and agony it takes to become a swordsmith." Before he left Houston to return home he presented the sword club with a *tonto* he made—an outstanding gesture for such a traditional man. If you're wondering why I have included Sensei Shigeharu in this book, it's simple: When you think of Japanese martial arts, you think of samurais. When you think of samurais, you think of swords and kendo, the way of the sword. Kendo is still the number one martial art in Japan today. So, Sensei Shigeharu may not be a martial artist, but his art is as old, if not older, than jujitsu, and it is as much a part of the Way of the Samurai as any technique. It must be respected and cherished for generations to come.

Top, Sensei Toru Iwahori, 7th Dan, from the Osaka Police Department, and All-Japan Champion, who gave a kendo and taiho jitsu clinic one fall at my dojo. Like most of the Japanese teachers who have come to my dojo, his taiho jitsu was outstanding. This photo is included because his class was most memorable. It took me approximately six weeks to recover from it; I was his uke.

Bottom, l. to r.: Sensei Masao Fukada (Instructor for Central Japan Police Schools; the top taiho kitsu instructor in Japan, besides being Central Japan's kendo sensei), a kendo student, Darrell Craig, and the Chief of Police (at the time this picture was taken he was Vice Chief of Police in Nagoya City), Sadamu Hiraiwa. (Sensei Masao Fukada has my deepest appreciation for his contribution to this manuscript. He sent me a great deal of taiho jitsu information and, without his help, many parts of this book would be incomplete.)

Left, l. to r.: Nagoya Castle Vice Chief Sadamu Hiraiwa, Darrell Craig, Chief of Police of Nagoya Shinpei Iznhara, and a stdent who accompanied me on this trip.

Below, l. to r.: Frank H. Goishi, head of Chiba Dojo in Fresno, California; Sensei Harutane Chiba, head of the Chiba Kendo Schools from 1924 to 1992 and head instructor for the Hokushin Ryu, now succeeded by his eldest son, Sensei Toshitane Chiba, our new leader; and Darrell Craig.

Above, l. to r.: Sensei Chiba, Darrell Craig, Sensei Bill Smith, and Bob Lawson at a clinic held by Sensei Chiba for the two U.S. dojos in Houston, Texas, and Fresno, California.

Left, Darrell Craig and teammates during the 1985 World Kendo Championships in Paris.

Above, The Houston Hoku-shin Kendo team in California at the 1992 National Championships, where they took third place: (*left to right*) Ryoichi Yamaji, Bob Lawson, Rick TheBerge, Gordon Small, Lanny Morton (team captain), and Kenichi Sooda.

Right, A clinic held at my dojo by Sensei Takeshi Nakamura (8th Dan Hanshi), and Sensei Tadanori Ota (8th Dan Kyoshi), and my son, Darren Craig, who has been involved in judo and kendo since he was five years old. Sensei Nakamura and Sensei Ota, two of the most outstanding, knowledgeable instructors I have ever met, head the Kaisho Police Department in Tokyo. When I asked Sensei Nakamura his police rank for a newspaper article, he said, "I don't have any rank. Sensei Ota and myself are similar to the Chief of Police and Assistant Chief for the Kaisho, and all we have is one little card stating this fact." Of course, neither of them needed any type of card; if you're a police officer in Japan, everyone knows who you are.

Above, Wendy Craig and Sensei Tadanori Ota at the farewell party in Houston, where we made Sensei Ota an honorary Texan. Wendy placed third in the 1987 Judo National Championships in San Diego, California.

Left, Sensei Yajima (my first kendo teacher) and Sensei Hata.

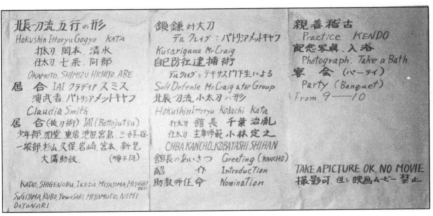

Top, Sensei Riki H. Kogure, who was Sensei Tomiki's uke for several years in Tomiki Aikido, and Sensei Hata.

Bottom, a poster in the Osaka Hombo Dojo. If you look closely, you can see that Claudia Smith was giving a demonstration in Iaido, and Bill Smith and Darrell Craig were demonstrating the use of the kusarigama. Note the part about no movies allowed.

Top, Sensei Chiba and Darrell Craig in 1979 at the grand opening of the first Hokushinkan Chiba Dojo outside of Japan.

Bottom, Darren Craig in 1980 at the Chiba Hombo Dojo in Osaka, Japan. He stayed that summer with Chiba Sensei and family to practice kendo.

Top, Osaka Police practicing taiho jitsu.
Bottom, The Japanese Police Academy just outside Osaka City during a shodan and nidan rank examination.

Top, Claudia Smith and Tommy Callaway demonstrating taiho jitsu techniques at the Texas Renaissance Festival. For about nine years I had a Japanese village in the center of the Renaissance Festival. It consisted of eight Japanese houses, a Japanese fortune booth, and a tea house. In the center was a large stage on which we gave five demonstrations per day in different martial arts. Callaway was involved in one of these demonstrations, where he portrayed a heckler in the audience saying things to his sister, Claudia—for example, "Oh, that wouldn't work against a real man." We finally invited him onto the stage, where he verbally challenged Claudia Smith and then (in a prearranged sequence) began a physical attack. This demonstration was so dynamic that the audience once thought it was real, and several men climbed onto the stage to protect Callaway. We had to stop the demonstration to settle the crowd down and explain that, in reality, they were sister and brother. Even after this, it took Mr. Callaway's personal assurance that it was a demonstration and that Claudia was truly his loving sister. To this day, I don't think everyone believed him, because no one could really understand a brother allowing his older sister to do such horrible things to a "little" brother.

Bottom, Tim Smith and Darrell Craig using taiho jitsu pressure techniques for a take-down at the Texas Renaissance Festival.

Above, Sensei Chiba carefully watching Claudia Smith and Darrell Craig demonstrating iai jitsu at a Japanese festival.

Right, Claudia Smith and Gary Grossman utilizing the happo-no-kuzushi chart (note the numbers on the floor) to practice kuzushi and tsukuri for tai otoshi.

> **"We shall not cease from exploring,**
> **And the end of all our exploring**
> **Will be to arrive where we start,**
> **And know the place for the first time."**
>
> —Old Proverb

CHAPTER SIX
Kansetsu Waza

OVER THE PAST three decades, I have worked in a teaching capacity with almost every known type of law enforcement agency. I have traveled with federal special forces units and taught my techniques around the globe. Once, I was even hired by two foreign countries to teach their special military police the PR24.

Policemen and special forces are basically the same all over the world—respected by some, reviled by others. I've liked working for law enforcement agencies because I think they are composed of a special breed of individuals, much like true dedicated martial artists. If you are in martial arts, someone always wants you to break a board; if you are in law enforcement, someone always wants you to fix a ticket.

I am dedicating this and the next couple of chapters to professional law enforcement officers. In this chapter, we will discuss four-suspect movement, or "come-along," techniques. But first, a bit of law enforcement personnel humor. A young man was traveling down a lonely country road. He came to a four-way stop. Not seeing anyone coming, he just slowed down and rolled through the intersection. He traveled only a few yards when—out of nowhere—flashing red lights appeared in his rearview mirror. He pulled over to the shoulder of the road. A large burly policeman got out of his patrol car and came up to the man's car. "Didn't you see that stop sign back there, son?" he asked. The young lad replied, "Yea, I saw it." The policeman inquired, "Then why didn't you stop?" The young lad looked up at the policeman and, with a sneer, replied, "Well, I almost stopped." Whereupon the policeman opened the car door and demanded that the young lad get out of the car. The policeman then removed his nightstick and started hitting the young man about the back and shoulders. He then proclaimed, "Now, do you want me to stop or to almost stop?"

Some type of enforcement of rules and regulations has existed as long as man has lived in a "civilized" state. In Japan during the Tokugawa period, one of the most famous police and customs stations was in the mountains between Kyoto, the old capital, and Edo, the new capital; it was called Hakone. Umemoto Sensei, head instructor for taiho

Figure 186A

Figure 186B

Figure 186C

Figure 186D

Figure 186E

Figure 186F

jitsu in Nagoya, told me that the most effective restraining techniques for use against reluctant samurai were developed at Hakone. There was no way to avoid this station when traveling between Kyoto and Edo. Its purpose was to control communication between the warlords and to restrict the samurais' movements, and each traveler had to have a special pass. Figure 186A shows the front of such a pass. On it is stated, "Customs License"; on the left side is a seal stating, "Issued by Hakone Customs." Figure 186B shows the reverse side, which reads:

> *To: All Customs Officers at Hakone Custom House*
>
> *Regarding this permission, it is limited to only one person. The person mentioned on the right has a valid reason to pass through Hakone. We want to ask Hakone Customs to pass him through your customs safely. For his future necessity, we certify the details mentioned on this tegata (customs permission).*
>
> > *May 27th, Keio 2nd year (1866)*
> > *Myoshu (Village Mayor)*

Figure 186C is a photograph of the customs officer in charge of the station. He was of samurai status. Figure 186D shows the guards, who were not of samurai descent. This photograph clearly shows the family crests (or, as we call them, coats of arms) of the three hundred Japanese feudal lords of the Tokugawa era. These enabled the guards or policemen to recognize a traveler's affiliation and therefore more quickly verify the information on the pass. In Figure 186E, we see the outside of the police station and, leaning against the outer wall, the police restraining device called a *sode garami* (sleeve entangler).

The sode garami was an extremely useful device for the policemen. Japanese police officers were not samurai, and only samurai could maim or kill another samurai. (A true samurai could kill anyone below his station for any reason without fear of punishment.) Accordingly, if a samurai decided to resist arrest, the arresting policeman's job was made very difficult. This is where the sode garami became a most important tool—even more so than a weapon—in a policeman's hands. As shown in the photograph, the sode garami has large nails or spikes surrounding the upper part. This enabled the policeman, once a samurai had drawn his sword (clearly an act of resistance), to entangle the samurai's long sleeves. Then, holding the samurai at bay, another officer would use his sode garami to entangle the samuri's hakama. Once these two garments were entangled, the policemen could force the samurai to the ground and pin his neck or arm with the sode garami shown in the center of Figure 186E. They would then proceed to tie the samurai in a taiho jutsu manner that we will discuss in Chapter Nine.

In Figure 186F, we find the *junte* (also known as the *jutte*), which was a forerunner of the now common police nightstick. The junte consisted of a wooden handle and an iron shaft approximately 11 inches long, with a prong varying in length on one side. The junte was used to capture the sword or restrain the samurai in a manner similar to that used with the nightstick. The outcome of a confrontation between a samurai and a policeman would depend entirely upon the proficiency of the practitioners. Keep in mind that a samurai was not necessarily the expert swordsman we see portrayed in the movies. Especially during the Tokugawa era (the late 1800s), a lot of men were samurai in name only. You could be born a samurai, you could be adopted by a samurai family, and—believe it or not—by this time you could even purchase a samurai title. So in a lot of circumstances, the confrontation was between a very professional policeman and an unprofessional samurai. But a policeman was not allowed to carry the long samurai sword called a *katana*. Accordingly, if he tried to restrain a true battle-hardened professional samurai or, in some cases, a *ronin* (a masterless samurai), he would surely meet his end.

I have set forth below four come-along techniques. They are of a standard type used in Japan for centuries and brought to the United States around the turn of this century. From time to time and from teacher to teacher, variations creep into each technique. The end result, however, is basically the same, and each is laudatory in its own right. But do not try to master them all; try them out and select the one that you feel is best suited to you. Then practice it until you become proficient at it. Always keep in mind that the most important element in making the technique work is the off-balancing of your suspect.

In all my travels and time spent with Japanese police, I have never heard a name for any of the following techniques. That doesn't mean they are unnamed, but no one I have trained with seems to know the names. Most of these techniques were developed by the jujitsu master at a police academy. Such a man had normally trained in several types of jujitsu or, after 1882, judo. These techniques have been refined and tested on the street time after time. These are the most commonly used techniques and the ones I try to focus on when teaching at police academies. They are a subset of *kansetsu waza*, or joint-locking techniques. For the sake of the reader, we will call them *ude waza*.

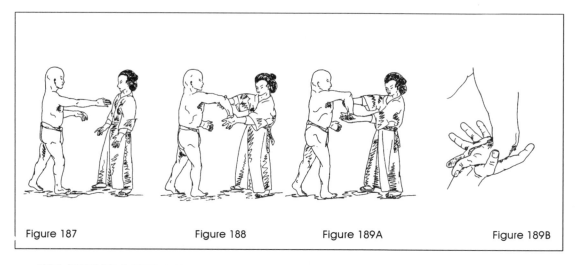

Figure 187   Figure 188   Figure 189A   Figure 189B

TECHNIQUE NUMBER 1: (*Ude-Garami*)

In Figure 187, tori is in the right forward posture with his back to the front of the happo-no-kuzushi chart. Uke (in this chapter we'll call him the "suspect") is facing him with his right foot and hand forward. (This technique can start as if the suspect is pushing you away or maybe even reaching to pull off your badge.)

As the suspect reaches forward with his right hand, tori quickly slides his right foot forward about six inches, seizes the suspect's right elbow with his right hand, and places his left hand at the top side of the suspect's right hand (Figure 188).

In Figure 189A, tori pulls forward with his right hand and pushes upward with his left hand, causing the suspect's arm to form a 90-degree angle and making him become off balance forward. Tori allows his left hand to pivot on the back of the suspect's right hand. Figure 189B is a close look at the position of tori's left hand on the suspect's right hand.

Figure 190

Figure 191

In Figure 190, tori places the suspect's right elbow between tori's left upper arm and his left side by continued pulling with his right hand toward line 2. The suspect will be off balance on his right little toe and will step to his right, probably with his right foot.

In Figure 191, tori applies pressure to the top of the suspect's hand; this pressure can be applied straight down with his left hand. Tori will get some type of reaction.

If the suspect tries to resist by reaching across with his left hand to grab the wrist lock (Figure 192), tori simply changes hands by taking hold of the suspect's fingers with his right hand. Tori then rotates his hand clockwise while placing his left thumb on the suspect's right wrist bone.

Figure 193 shows a variation of this technique. It is performed by turning the suspect's hand over so that his palm is facing upward then prying down with your right hand on his fingers. You can dislocate the wrist and/or the fingers if you apply too much pressure. Remember, the job of a good policeman is to arrest the suspect, not to punish him.

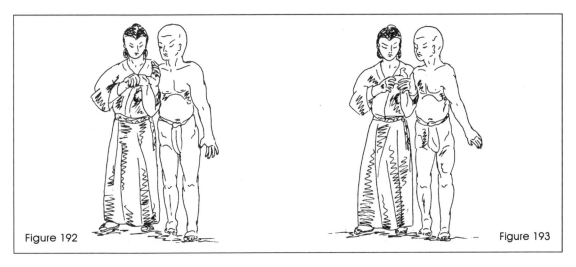

Figure 192

Figure 193

TECHNIQUE NUMBER 2: (*Ude-Gatame*)

Again, tori is standing with his back to the front of the happo-no-kuzushi chart and the suspect is facing him. The suspect reaches out with his right hand and tori seizes it with his left (Figure 194). [*Note:* In some cases, the officer will already have hold of the suspect's wrist. In this drawing, tori has hold of the back of the suspect's hand; I prefer to have hold of the suspect's wrist.]

While turning the suspect's wrist counterclockwise so that the palm is facing up and the elbow is toward the floor, tori steps to line 2 with his left foot allowing his right foot to pivot naturally toward line 7 (Figure 195). As his hips pivot, tori pulls forward with his right hand toward line 1. The suspect will resist by pulling backward and will be off-balance on line 5. While this is taking place, tori keeps the elbow straight and steps with his left foot to line 4 while changing the suspect's wrist into his right hand.

As the suspect leans forward (Figure 196), tori smashes the back of his hand into the suspect's groin. Tori continues moving and places the suspect's wrist between his legs so that the top of the suspect's elbow rests in his groin area. Immediately, tori takes hold of the wrist with both hands and lifts upward (Figure 197). The suspect will be off-balance forward. It is important at this point not to use too much strength, or the suspect will do a somersault forward. Tori continues applying pressure upward with his left hand and seizes the suspect's hair with his right hand, keeping his head up (Figure 198). If the suspect is bald or has short hair, tori simply takes his free hand and grips the top of the suspect's left eye socket. (Be careful not to poke the eye itself.) Tilt the suspect's head to your right.

This technique will allow you to move the suspect quickly and quietly out of a crowd. Most of all, it amuses and quiets the crowd. One variation of this technique involves simply grabbing the back of the suspect's collar or belt. Another involves keeping both hands on the suspect's wrist and moving him at a slower pace. Still another (useful with a troublesome suspect) involves moving to the same side of the arm you are holding between his legs. Taking your free hand, you place it under the suspect's neck, lift upward slowly with both hands, and move the suspect sideways to the awaiting rendezvous.

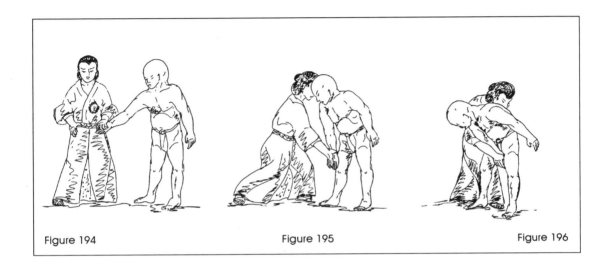

Figure 194   Figure 195   Figure 196

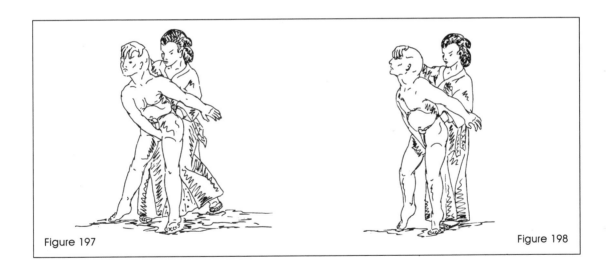

Figure 197   Figure 198

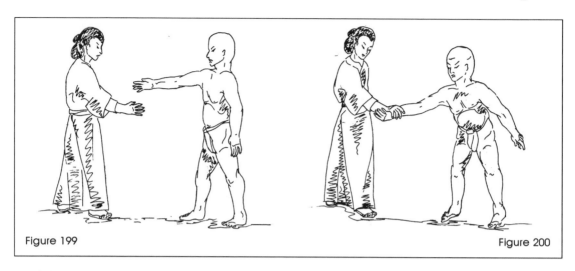

Figure 199

Figure 200

TECHNIQUE NUMBER 3: (*Ude-Gatame*)

In Figure 199, tori is facing the front of the happo-no-kuzushi chart. He is straddling line 5, in a right forward posture. The suspect reaches out with his right hand.

Figures 200, 201, and 202 involve a continuous walking movement on line 4. In Figure 200, tori reaches with his right hand to the suspect's wrist and turns it counterclockwise so that the palm is facing up and the elbow is toward the ground. Tori pulls gently downward and toward the end of line 4.

In Figure 201, tori steps across his body with his left foot to line 4. He continues rotating the suspect's wrist counterclockwise, while placing his left arm over and in front of the suspect's chest, then under his right arm just above the elbow.

Figure 202 shows the completion of the technique. Tori reaches around and grips the top of his own right forearm with his left hand. He keeps pressure on the suspect's elbow by pushing downward with his right hand and upward with his left forearm, much like a vise.

[*Note:* If you're trying to learn this technique by just looking at the pictures, you're going to have a very hard time with Figure 202 because it shows the suspect's hand incorrectly (or just before it's turned counterclockwise); the palm should be facing up. A uniformed officer must always remain aware of the position of his "Sam Brown." Thus, I do not recommend this technique in all situations.]

Figure 201

Figure 202

TECHNIQUE NUMBER 4:
(*Ude Garami* with *Hadaka Jime*)

This come-along incorporates an arm bar with a restraining technique about the neck. The two in combination are impregnable. When practicing this technique, you must be extremely careful and pay strict attention to each and every movement. If your training partner is large and stocky, like a bodybuilder, you will have to constantly release pressure on his right shoulder to complete the technique, for it is very, very easy to dislocate his elbow, shoulder, or neck. I might also point out that, in some law enforcement academies, this combination technique is strictly forbidden.

In Figure 203, tori has his back toward the front of the chart; he is in a left forward posture; the suspect is facing him in a right forward posture. Again, this technique can be accomplished by having hold on the suspect's wrist instead of waiting for him to attack you.

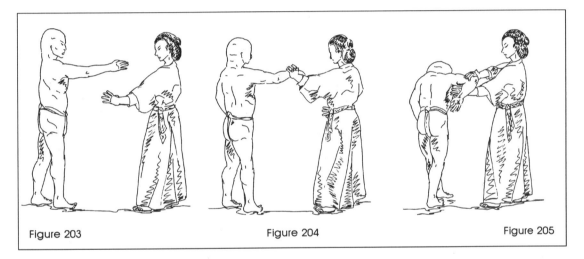

Figure 203   Figure 204   Figure 205

In either case, as contact is made with tori's left hand, tori moves his right foot slightly to his right rear toward line 8 (Figure 204). Tori takes hold of the suspect's right wrist with his left hand and pulls downward, thus breaking the suspect's balance to line 8.

With the suspect's balance broken toward line 8, tori reaches with his right hand to the back of the suspect's right elbow and continues pulling toward line 8 while allowing his left hand to rotate on the back of the suspect's wrist.

Figure 206 shows the continuation of the motion in Figure 205. Tori keeps the suspect off balance by using the back of his right hand to push the suspect's shoulder downward.

In Figure 207, tori has now moved his left hand up to the top of the suspect's right shoulder. He forms a fist with his right hand and places his thumb on top of his index finger so that his thumb is bent upward and firm.

In Figure 208, tori then places his thumb under the suspect's right ear and jawbone, rakes it leftward across the suspect's throat, and pushes down on the suspect's right shoulder with his left forearm. Tori keeps his right hand moving across the suspect's neck until he is standing directly behind the suspect. With his right hand, tori takes hold of the suspect's left shoulder.

If you have trouble correctly concluding this technique, remember to release some of the pressure on the suspect's right shoulder. Also, do not stand on your toes; rather,

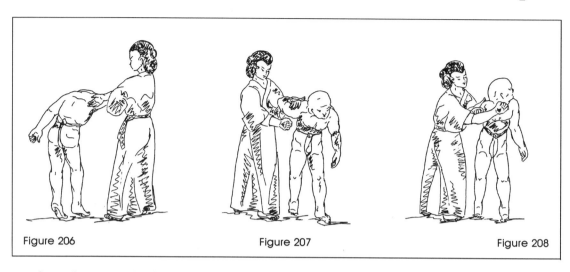

Figure 206   Figure 207   Figure 208

force the suspect backward so that you always remain taller than he, regardless of his real height. It is most important to keep the suspect off balance at all times when performing this technique.

Referring back to Figure 207, if you have difficulty controlling the suspect's shoulder, try the "shoulder pinch." This is done by pressing your thumb into the top front side of the suspect's shoulder while maintaining your grip with your fingers at the back of his shoulder. This is a hypersensitive area. With a small amount of practice, you will be able to locate it easily. Remember that the ball of the thumb should dig in at the point where the head of the upper arm joins the scapula. Very often this pressure alone will make the suspect move about as you desire. The suspect is frequently lying facedown; so, it is easy to pressure this sensitive area in a severe manner. The suspect will find the pain so intense that he will roll over in order to weaken the force of the technique. This sensitive area can also be attacked with the fist. The effect of the blow will cause numbness to the suspect's arm. In a crowded or narrow passageway, an officer confronted by an obstinate suspect who will not allow the officer to pass can apply the technique from behind on both shoulders while pushing the suspect ahead of him. The suspect will then go in the desired direction. The same technique can be applied to someone you wish to eject from the premises.

This concludes Chapter Six. Keep in mind the advice to find one come-along technique that best suits you, and practice it until you become proficient.

> **"Both the slayer
> And the slain
> Are like a dew-drop
> and a flash of lightning;
> They are thus to be regarded."**
>
> —The last words of
> a Japanese warrior (1656)

CHAPTER SEVEN
Resisting a Handgun

OF THE THREE techniques in this chapter, one addresses a threat from the front and two address threats from the rear. Based upon my experience in law enforcement, I believe the rear attacks are most likely to be made in two situations: attempted hostage taking and attempted robbery or kidnapping by multiple attackers.

It should go without saying that one does not use a real gun in practicing these techniques. In this regard, I shall share a personal memory that may be helpful in dealing with your ego. I call it "The Ego and the Arrow."

About sixteen years ago, I was preparing to put on a demonstration at a local television station. I wanted to present something completely different from anything most people had ever seen. My youthful background in show business had taught me that it was a good rule of thumb to have a child doing a hard stunt or a female getting the upper hand with a male. With this in mind, I asked a female student, Claudia Smith, to be my partner.

Of course, her first question was "What do I have to do?" I replied, "Your husband tells me that you're involved in competitive archery. It's quite simple. All you have to do is stand thirty or forty feet away and shoot me with an arrow." By the expression on her face I could tell she was thinking, "You have got to be kidding." Applying my sensei powers of persuasion, I explained to her that I had been studying the art of iaido (the art of drawing the sword) and that I would simply draw the sword from the scabbard and cut the arrow in half before it reached me.

She questioned me: for example, "Have you done this before?" and "What happens if you miss?" At that point, with a little roughness in my voice, I said, "Look, do you want to do this demonstration with me or not? You have to trust me. I have lots of experience, and besides, I'm only going to use a thirty-five-pound bow." Although I hadn't really convinced her, she was perhaps afraid to say no to her teacher, so she agreed. We arranged to meet Saturday at the school to rehearse.

On Saturday afternoon, I explained to Claudia how it was all going to work. I had purchased an arrow designed for shooting birds. It had huge feathers and was, therefore, supposedly incapable of traveling as fast as a regular arrow—and, of course, it did not have a hunting tip on the end! I explained that she would stand at the far side of the dojo and point dead center at my chest. When I gave the command "Now!" she would release the arrow. All I had to do was simply quickly pull my samurai sword and cut the arrow. I could tell I was gaining her confidence; now we both believed that I could do it.

She took her position and aimed the arrow. I repeated, "You understand completely that you do not release the arrow until I plainly say 'Now'?" She confirmed by shaking her head affirmatively. We took our positions again. As I looked straight at the head of the arrow, a tiny thought appeared, "What happens if I do miss?" The answer was absolutely astounding. Being the excellent student that she was, she was probably going to shoot that arrow right through me. So I held up my hand and said, "Let's wait a minute. I have an idea." Back in those days, the dojo was behind a convenience store, so I told her I was going there for a moment. When I returned, she saw I had purchased a two-and-a-half-inch round rubber ball. I explained that, for safety reasons (not that I ever thought I couldn't do the technique), I was going to place the ball on the end of the arrow. With its large feathers and weighted by the ball, the arrow would slow down even more, and the feat would be even more easily accomplished.

As we took up our action stations, I was once again facing the arrow, when I had my second thought of wisdom. What if I miss, and the arrow hits with such impact that it goes through the ball and into me? Once again I stopped the proceedings. I explained to Claudia that—not for my protection but solely for her peace of mind—I was going to put on a karate chest protector. I remember distinctly her looking at me with her head tilted to one side. She never uttered a word—after all, I was the sensei—but she must have thought that this was the first intelligent thing I'd done all day.

As we proceeded to our appointed positions again, I had more confidence than ever, knowing that if I accidentally missed my mark (which would be virtually impossible), I wouldn't wind up in the hospital. Taking a ready stance with my left foot to the rear, my right hand on the handle of sword, and, looking the archer squarely in the eye, I said the magic word, "Now!" Thud! the arrow hit me squarely in the chest.

"Claudia, I said not to release the arrow until I give the command," I exclaimed. She said absolutely nothing, but I could see a thin smile on her face. "Let's do it again," I said. "This time wait until I say 'Now.'" I handed her the arrow and walked back to my position, thinking, "Maybe this isn't going to be as easy as I thought. It surely can't be that I'm not as good as I think I am, so I'll do the most logical thing; I'll cheat. I'll pull the sword halfway out of the scabbard before I tell her to shoot."

Back on our marks, everything ready, the sword half out of the scabbard, body relaxed, eyes focused on the arrow: "Now!" At this point, I can't really remember whether the arrow or "Now" came first. Nevertheless, before the sword could come out, the arrow had hit the mark again. I couldn't believe this was happening to me. How humiliating, being shot twice in exactly the same spot by a student who wasn't even a black belt!

Picking the arrow up from the floor and looking for my ego—which must have been so big a blind man could see it—I motioned Claudia closer. As she approached, I assured her, with a smile that it wasn't her fault, but said that there had to be a way to accomplish this feat. I decided at this time that the problem lay in removing the sword from the scabbard: it took too much time. So the solution was very simple. I explained to her that this time I would have the sword completely out of the scabbard in the *chudan*, or center posture, so there could not be any possible way to miss hitting the arrow with it. I even took a piece of chalk and made an X on my chest protector so she had something to aim at and, most importantly, so that I would know where the arrow would hit. It's hard to believe, but this made perfectly good sense to both of us at the time. Taking up positions, confidence back, shoulders relaxed, I uttered the magic word. Before I could even see the arrow, I felt the thud.

I could go on with this story, but it would be pointless because the conclusion was always the same. Some years later, Chiba Sensei explained to me how he had seen the technique demonstrated in Japan. First, it was never performed with a katana in a scabbard, but always with a *boken* (wooden sword). Second, the archer never aimed at his opponent, for the simple reason that a person cannot focus his eyes on an arrow coming straight at him. The feat is accomplished by shooting the arrow over the person's head, allowing the person to focus on the shaft of the arrow rather than the point. Chiba Sensei stated that he thought there was only one ryu or family martial clan in Japan that performed this feat, and he was sure that the technique had been handed down from generation to generation. Sensei stated that, if I was really interested in learning the trick, he would make some inquiries and the next time I was in Japan he would introduce me to the ryu's sensei. I quickly replied, "No thank you, Sensei."

I hope you can learn from my experience. If you feel it is absolutely necessary to practice gun techniques with something other than a wooden gun, use a plastic spring-loaded rubber suction dart pistol, the kind you can find in toy stores. Getting hit with the toy dart will bring forcefully home to you the necessity for quicker and more skillful execution of the technique. Remember: the velocity of that toy dart is but a tiny fraction of that of a bullet.

There are three points I would like to make about the following techniques. First, keep in mind that money and valuables can be replaced and that the chance of success of any technique like these is, at best, fifty-fifty—and then only if the defender is skilled in its execution. In a real situation, the chance of success will depend entirely on the defender's subconscious, not his conscious, state of mind. Second, I do not show a final conclusion to these techniques, such as a kick to the groin or poke to the eye. The reason is that, once you secure the weapon, I hope you'll run. Most important, I hope you'll do whatever your subconscious designates at that point. Third, these techniques can be performed right or left simply by reversing the movements.

TECHNIQUE NUMBER 1

In Figure 209, the attacker is holding the pistol in his right hand, pointing it somewhere in the vicinity of your stomach or chest. It makes no difference whether his right foot or his left foot is forward. In a picturesque type of situation, he may say, "Put up your hands." Never raise your hands above your head. Simply raise your forearms up leaving the elbow at the waist and your hands at elbow level. If he says "Hands higher," simply raise your hands upward, leaving your elbows in place. Your hands are now approximately even with your shoulders.

As shown in Figure 210, with the gun pointing at your chest, pivot 90 degrees clockwise on the balls of both feet. Be sure you have not reached for the gun but rather that you have removed your body from the muzzle. Simultaneously, lower your left hand thereby striking the attacker's forearm with your left forearm and moving the attacker's arm above and approximately in front of his left foot.

Reach with your right hand to the back of the attacker's gun hand (Figures 211 and 212). Once you have his fist firmly in your grip, twist his wrist toward him while simultaneously pivoting your feet back to their original position. The weapon should now be pointing directly at the attacker.

To conclude the technique (Figure 213), simply reach with your left hand, palm down, grab the weapon by the muzzle, and twist counterclockwise until the attacker releases his grip.

TECHNIQUE NUMBER 2

This technique involves a typical hostage situation. My experience in law enforcement indicates that the most useful technique in these situations is patience. In helping to accomplish this end, I suggest that my students think of the state name "Texas" (or, if you're from Tennessee, think of "Tennessee") three times. The key is the "T." The first *Texas* stands for "talk." Talk creates time. Even if your assailant tells you to shut up, you are communicating. In a hostage situation, the assailant generally wants something, and communication opens the door to discovering what it is. The second *Texas* stands for "time." Time is most important. It possibly allows other people to see what is going on and to get help. More importantly, time is something the assailant has little of. The third *Texas* stands for "technique." Even if the technique involves nothing but talk and time, it may be the proper technique to use. If you feel that you're going to be killed and you have absolutely nothing to lose, then you might try one of the following techniques.

In Technique Number 2, we find the attacker standing behind you with the pistol placed at the base of your skull. He may or may not be holding you with his left hand. For our purposes, we'll have the attacker place his left hand somewhere in the vicinity of your left elbow (Figure 214).

The first motion in this technique is to turn your head to your right almost to the point at which your chin is touching your right shoulder (Figure 215). Then simultaneously raise your right forearm up to where your hand is even with your right shoulder while pivoting 90 degrees clockwise on the balls of your feet so that your left foot is directly behind your right heel.

Move your left foot clockwise to line 4, in front of your right foot, and strike the forearm of your attacker's gun hand with your right forearm. As shown in Figure 216, continue pivoting to your right, simultaneously bringing your left hand in front of your

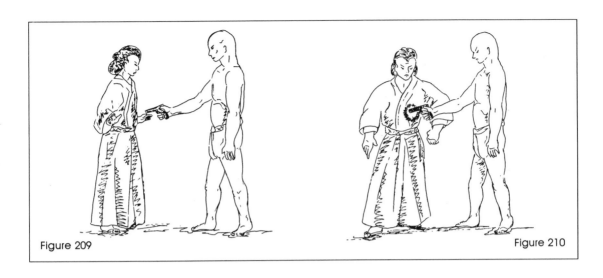

Figure 209

Figure 210

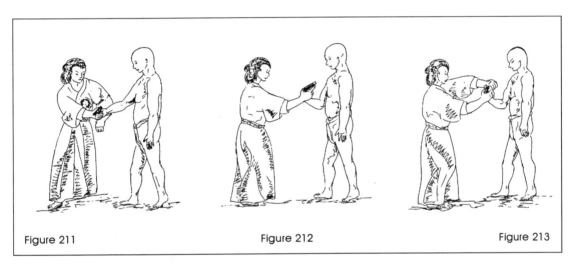

Figure 211

Figure 212

Figure 213

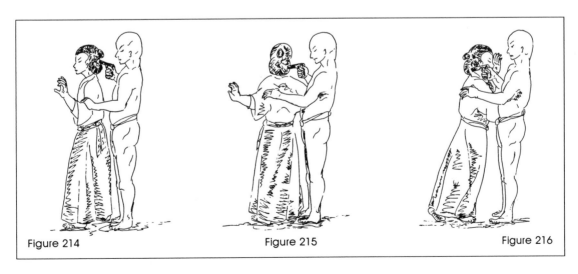

Figure 214

Figure 215

Figure 216

body and taking a firm grip on the attacker's gun hand wrist with your right hand.

Place your left arm over the attacker's right shoulder, sliding it down to his elbow (Figure 217). Twist the attacker's wrist counterclockwise with your right hand until his elbow is pointing straight up. At this point secure the attacker's wrist with your left hand, palm facing down. Step 90 degrees with your left foot, pushing down with your left forearm and twisting counterclockwise with your left hand. Reach with your right hand to the weapon and move the muzzle away from you (Figure 218).

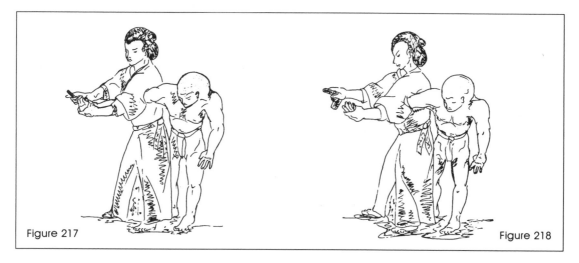

Figure 217

Figure 218

TECHNIQUE NUMBER 3

I have left the most complicated technique to the last partially because there can be so many beginning variations. Whenever I teach this technique at law enforcement academies, I always receive the "what if" questions. For example: What if he holds the gun to your neck? What if he holds the gun under your chin? What if he holds the gun up your nose? I can only say that after discussions with numerous federal and local special weapons and tactics groups, I have come to the conclusion that the following would be the most common situation for which to practice this technique.

As shown in Figure 219, the attacker is standing to your rear with the gun in his right hand placed approximately under your right ear. Turn your head quickly to the right and down (Figure 220), thereby bringing your right shoulder upward until its meets your chin. Simultaneously, raise your right arm so that it is parallel with the ground, keeping pressure on the gun with your chin and shoulder. At the Figure 219 and 220 stages, a lot of cadets ask, "What if, when you twist your head quickly and the gun is cocked, it fires? Won't it burst your eardrum?" My reply, "If you hear it go off, continue with the technique. If you don't hear it go off, you won't need to continue."

Reach up with your left hand, keeping your elbow pointing toward the floor (Figure 221). Twisting your upper torso to your right, place your left hand on the back of the attacker's gun hand and seize it, thereby controlling the hand and the weapon in a tight grip (Figure 222). Slide your right arm, palm up, just behind the attacker's right elbow.

Move the attacker's gun hand to your right (Figure 223), so that the muzzle of the gun crosses in front of his face. Seize the gun with your waiting open right hand.

Figure 219   Figure 220

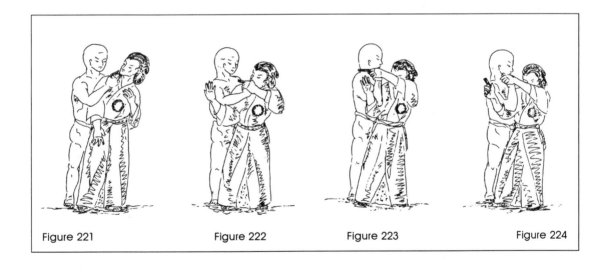

Figure 221   Figure 222   Figure 223   Figure 224

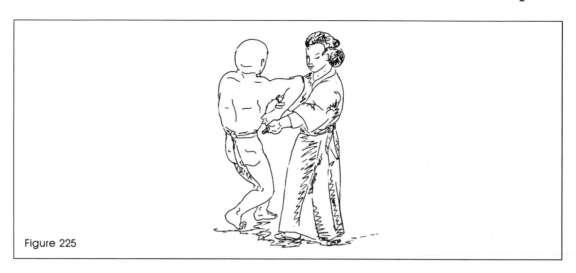

Figure 225

Continue this motion by pivoting 90 degrees to your right. Then take a step with your left foot straight forward or slightly to your right, whichever is more natural. Pull down against the attacker's thumb with your left hand, and take possession of the weapon with your right (Figure 224).

Figure 225 shows another conclusion of this technique. Once you get to Figure 225, simply pull straight down on the attacker's forearm, thereby dislocating his elbow.

In concluding this chapter, I want to reiterate a few points. First, never practice the techniques described in this chapter with real weapons. Second, recognize that these techniques are "techniques of last resort"; that is, they should be utilized when your life is at stake and no other exit avenue is apparent. Third, remember that the odds of successful completion are problematic at best. Therefore, the best "technique" I can recommend to you is to remain constantly vigilant so that the situations these techniques are intended to address never arise.

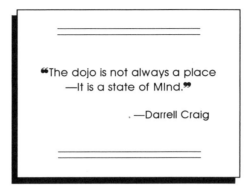

"The dojo is not always a place
—It is a state of Mind."

. —Darrell Craig

CHAPTER EIGHT
Hostage Situations and Kubudo

HOSTAGE SITUATIONS

IN THE FIRST part of this chapter, let us address certain types of knife attacks from the front and the back. In my law enforcement experience, I find these attacks to be most widely experienced in two situations: hostage taking and multiple attackers.

The following techniques are demonstrated in the right-hand attack mode; they can be performed in a left-hand attack mode simply by reversing the described moves. However, keep in mind that the majority of the world's population is right-handed—for example, 99 percent of all Japanese males are right-handed. This stems from the Japanese feudal days and the way of the samurai. The samurai class would go to extreme measures to assure that a boy would be right-handed, even when his left hand seemed dominant. They would immediately restrain the dominant left hand, forcing the young male to follow the true path of the samurai—that is, being right-handed. I often wonder how confusing it must have been to fight a left-handed samurai, given that all techniques (according to my Japanese sources) were taught using the right hand. I often suspect that Shinmen Musashi No Kami Fujiwara No Genshin, or as he is commonly known, Miyamoto Musashi, was ambidextrous. This would explain his lifelong desire to discover a way to use a sword in each hand completely independently of the other. It is ironic that, over the course of his life, in more than sixty victories, he never actually dueled with two swords.

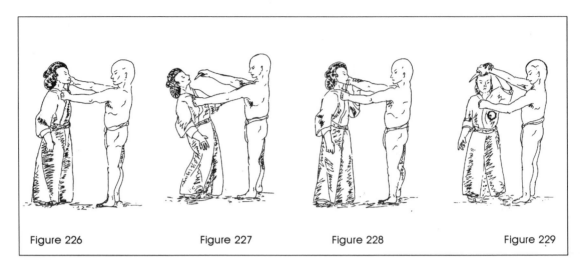

Figure 226   Figure 227   Figure 228   Figure 229

TECHNIQUE NUMBER 1

In Figure 226, the attacker holds the knife in his right hand, with the cutting edge to your throat. With his left hand he grasps your collar or jacket. Without moving your feet, lift your chin quickly so that your eyes are looking straight at the ceiling (Figure 227). Simultaneously, thrust into the attacker's throat with your left hand, using your fingertips like a spear.

As shown in Figure 228, the most common response is for the defender to reach with his right or left hand and to try to pull the knife away from his throat. *This is totally incorrect.* You can practice this motion and find out for yourself (naturally, using a wooden knife). Have the attacker press the wooden knife against your throat as soon as he sees you move your right or left hand. No matter how you try, the attacker will "cut" your throat before you can dislodge the knife. Moving backward first is the only way to escape.

Once you have completed the motions depicted in Figure 227, immediately move your right foot to your right, simultaneously reach with your left hand, palm up, to the attacker's right wrist, then twist clockwise (Figure 229).

Step forward with your left foot at a 45-degree angle to your left front, place your left elbow on the attacker's right elbow, and push directly down. When you have broken the

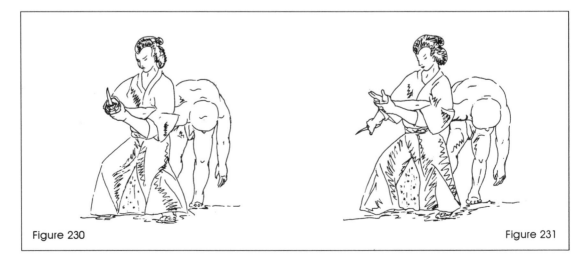

Figure 230   Figure 231

attacker's balance forward, quickly slide the attacker's elbow into your left armpit. Figure 230 shows this motion in its completion.

In Figure 230, you disarm the attacker by simply placing your right thumb on the attacker's right thumbnail and applying pressure toward the center of his palm. This will force his hand to open, thereby allowing you to easily remove the knife with your right hand.

Figure 232   Figure 233

TECHNIQUE NUMBER 2

In Figure 232, the attacker has the knife in his right hand, holding you firmly from behind with his left hand to your left upper side. The cutting edge of the knife is to the left side of your neck.

As shown in Figure 233, turn your head quickly about 45 degrees to your right. Simultaneously raise your right hand straight up and press your chin firmly down on the attacker's right forearm. When applied simultaneously these two motions will momentarily lock the attacker's arm in place. Continue this motion, and keep reaching upward with your right hand (Figure 234). Simultaneously reach for the attacker's right wrist with your left hand and swing your right leg in a crescent motion 180 degrees to your left,

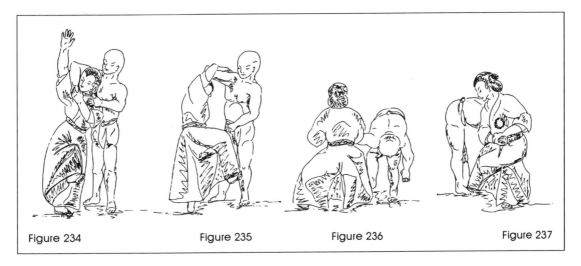

Figure 234   Figure 235   Figure 236   Figure 237

turning your head continuously toward the attacker's chest as you do so. Once you have freed yourself, your body position will be face-to-face with your attacker (Figure 235). Reach over the attacker's right shoulder with your right hand as your right foot comes to a stop on the floor.

In Figure 236, the attacker's right elbow should be facing upward; place your right elbow on it. Push immediately downward to the floor with your elbow while grasping the attacker's right wrist with your left hand. There will be a slight shift with your feet to your left owing to the off-balancing of the attacker.

Place the attacker's right elbow under your right armpit (Figure 237). Simultaneously, pull up with your left hand and press down with your right shoulder. Remove the knife in the same manner as in the conclusion of Technique Number 1.

Figure 238

Figure 239

TECHNIQUE NUMBER 3

This technique, though similar to Technique Number 2, has an entirely different conclusion. In Figure 238, we find the attacker again holding you from the rear but, instead of having the knife close to your throat, it is somewhere in the vicinity of your solar plexus. The attacker's left forearm holds your left elbow firmly.

Simultaneously step straight back with your left foot and push backward with your left elbow (Figure 239). While these two moves are taking place, push your right hand straight up until it is parallel to the floor.

As shown in Figure 240, move your right foot 180 degrees counterclockwise to your left. Pivot on your left foot and reach with your left hand to the attacker's right wrist. While your body is turning, reach up and secure the attacker's right hand with your right hand, still holding firmly with your left hand. Step to the rear with your left foot. You should now be facing your attacker (Figure 241). With the attacker's right wrist firmly in your hands, twist to your left and push upward, maintaining a 90-degree angle with the attacker's elbow and forearm.

Be sure the knife is pointing toward the attacker (Figure 242). Release a small amount of the tension on the wrist and slide your right foot forward and to the center of your attacker's feet. Give a quick upward motion to the attacker's wrist. As he feels the threat of the knife coming toward him he will take a step back and lean his head to the rear. This will allow you to thrust the knife into the attacker's throat.

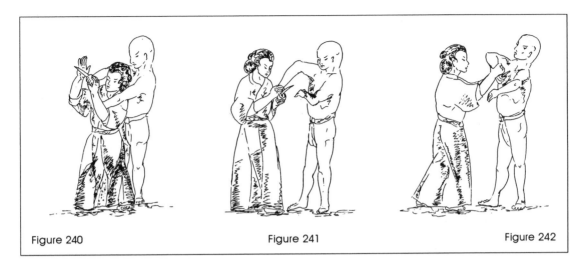

Figure 240   Figure 241   Figure 242

KUBUDO

Kubudo involves self-defense against weapons and the use of weapons as a defense. To begin this part of Chapter Eight, I would like to introduce a *tanto kata* (short sword) taken from the Kaisho Taiho Jitsu tactics. This kata consists of four basic knife attacks:

- *tsuki-kake*—stomach thrust
- *yoko-hidari-do*—left side cut
- *suri-age*—head thrust
- *yoko-migi-do*—right side cut

It is very foolish to practice with any type of sharp instrument. Therefore, I highly recommend using a wooden knife or Japanese tanto.

KATA 1: (*Tsuki-kake*)

As shown in Figure 243, uke holds the knife in his right hand and lunges forward with his right hand and foot, trying to thrust the knife at tori's stomach. Tori stands with his

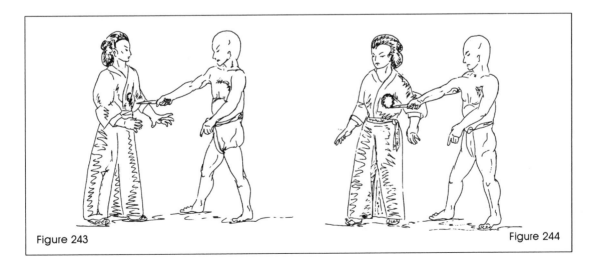

Figure 243   Figure 244

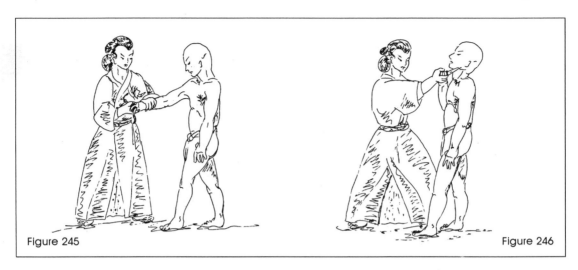

Figure 245   Figure 246

left foot forward; both hands are slightly below his waist.

As uke reaches the point of penetration, tori pivots on his left foot, bringing his right foot parallel with his left foot, approximately shoulder-distance apart (Figure 244). Simultaneously, tori blocks uke's wrist with his left upper forearm.

Once tori has escaped the thrust, he immediately moves his right foot back to the position in Figure 243, taking hold of uke's right forearm with his left hand as he does so (Figure 245). Tori takes hold of the back side of uke's hand with his right hand, pulls with his left hand and pushes with his right hand, thereby forcing the knife to be pointed toward uke's throat (Figure 246). Tori can either cut uke with the knife or proceed to twist uke's wrist counterclockwise with his right hand until uke releases the knife or falls to the ground.

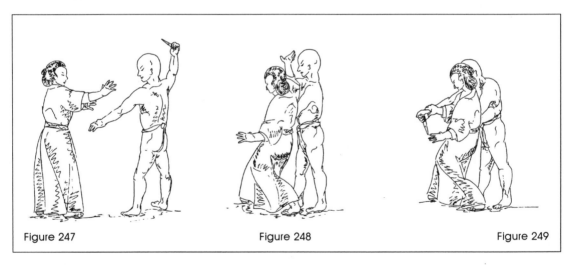

Figure 247   Figure 248   Figure 249

KATA 2: (*Suri-age*)

In this kata, uke holds the knife over his head in his right hand with his left foot forward as if to thrust down into tori's chest (Figure 247). Tori stands in a right-foot-forward posture, with his hands in a *jodan-no-kamai,* or high posture.

As uke steps forward with his right foot and thrusts straight down with the knife, tori pivots 180 degrees counterclockwise on his right foot, bringing his left foot to his back and to the side of uke's left leg (Figure 248). At the same time, tori raises his right hand up and to the center of uke's face. As the knife continues its forward circle, tori slides his right hand forward and on top of uke's wrist but does not allow the attacking arm to stop its downward motion (Figure 249).

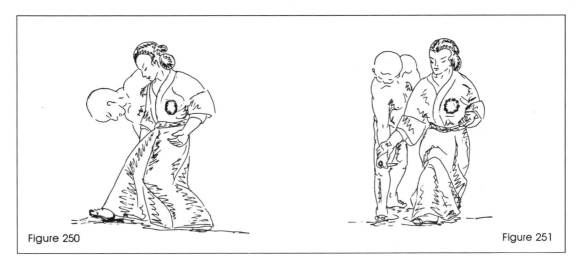

Figure 250

Figure 251

In Figures 250 and 251, tori slides his left foot still farther straight back and places his left knee on the ground, allowing uke's attacking hand to continue moving in a circle until the knife has penetrated uke's own body. [*Note:* In practicing this kata, uke should take a forward somersault fall to prevent injury.]

KATA 3: (*Yoko-hidari-do*)

This attack starts with the knife in uke's right hand, held slightly below waist level and slightly to the right rear (Figure 252). Tori stands in a right-foot-forward posture, with his hands in a chudan-no-kamai, or center, posture. Uke steps forward with his right foot and slashes horizontally at tori's left side.

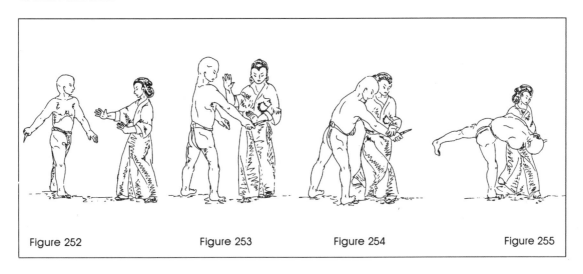

Figure 252　　　　Figure 253　　　　Figure 254　　　　Figure 255

In Figure 253, as uke continues to travel to his target, tori pivots on his right foot, moving his left foot 90 degrees counterclockwise. Tori's left hand blocks uke's wrist and pushes forward. As uke's balance is broken to his right front corner (Figure 254), tori continues to pivot on his right foot, thereby moving his left foot an additional 45 degrees counterclockwise, simultaneously raising his right hand just above his right shoulder.

In Figure 255, tori's right hand strikes the left side of uke's neck just below the ear. [*Note:* At this point, for kata purposes, tori should release uke's wrist and allow uke to take a right-forward fall.]

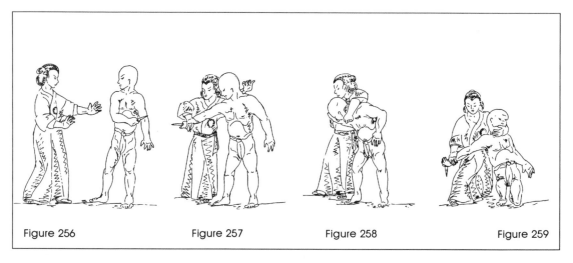

Figure 256   Figure 257   Figure 258   Figure 259

KATA 4: (*Yoko-migi-do*)

In this final knife kata, uke holds the knife in his right hand (Figure 256). His right forearm is across his body, and the knife is to his left side. Tori stands in a left-foot-forward posture, hands in chudan-no-kamai. Uke starts the attack by stepping forward with his right foot, then slashes horizontally at tori's right side.

Just before uke can cut tori's right side, but with uke's arm still in motion, tori pivots on his left foot, bringing the right foot clockwise 45 degrees, and catches uke's attacking arm with his right hand (Figure 257). Tori's left hand proceeds up and around uke's neck.

With uke's right arm extended, tori quickly brings uke's elbow into a locked position at tori's stomach. In Figure 258, tori continues reaching around and under uke's neck and chin with his left hand. Tori pushes up under uke's chin and brings the back of uke's head to tori's left shoulder.

Once uke has lost his balance backward, tori pushes straight down with his left forearm on the area between uke's left shoulder and neck (Figure 259) causing uke to fall to a kneeling or sitting position. Tori steps back with his left leg and places his left knee on the ground, keeping uke's right arm straight and his elbow locked and pointing down. Tori places and then breaks uke's right arm across his right knee. [*Note:* Breaking is obviously only for actual combat.] You should apply pressure against the elbow slowly while pulling uke's chin up and toward you, thereby forcing uke to submit and drop the knife. Immediately slide your right foot over the knife and drag it toward you.

Keep in mind that these four wazas are performed in an uninterrupted manner and should be practiced as such. The effect is to create one kata. Thus, uke should get to his feet quickly after each fall and begin the next attack. These wazas may also be practiced on the left side by reversing the stances.

> **"**As something of divinity enters
> into the making of the sword,
> its owner and user ought also to
> respond to the inspiration.
> He ought to be a spiritual man,
> not an agent of brutality.**"**
>
> —Emperor Ichijo (986–1011)

CHAPTER NINE
Hojo-Jutsu

HOJO-JUTSU IS mainly a lost art except at military or law enforcement agencies in Japan. There are approximately 133 rope-tying techniques. I am familiar with seven of these, and, although I believe that this art deserves a book dedicated totally to it, I am including here only two of the simpler techniques. Each was taught to me by a sensei from the Kaisho Police Department. I owe so much to these wonderful senseis that to name any one would require me to name them all, and that would take a chapter in itself. So let me take this opportunity to thank every sensei who gave so unselfishly of his time and knowledge. My only regret is that some of these great senseis have now passed away and their knowledge is forever lost.

About 1927 Sensei Takaji Shimizu from the Itatsu Ryu demonstrated the working principle of hojo-jutsu to the Japanese police commission. By virtue of Sensei Shimizu's demonstration of how to immobilize an aggressor by using a cord, the police officials adopted several techniques for use in controlling prisoners. Police training methods of hojo-jutsu were being constantly revised until approximately 1932. My understanding is that at that time Sensei Shimizu became the sole hojo instructor of the Tokyo police. He immediately organized hojo instruction for all military and law enforcement agencies. After World War II, Sensei again revised his cord-tying methods and made them more suitable for use in today's society.

Itatsu Ryu, which is a seventeenth-century classical bujutsu, forms the basis from which the Japanese police teach all their modern tying techniques. A Japanese policeman is trained to apprehend and tie a number of suspects entirely by himself. In order to utilize hojo-jutsu, one must be able to subdue the attacker quickly and keep him under total control; this in itself takes a great deal of training. Thus, in learning hojo-jutsu, a Japanese policeman also learns *torito*, the Japanese art of seizing and restraining a suspect. As a result, hojo-jutsu in the Kaisho consists of five fundamentals using the tying cord, four techniques of *inchi-nawa* (tying from the rear), and three techniques of *hoshu-nawa* (tying from the front). The most commonly used hojo techniques in police work today

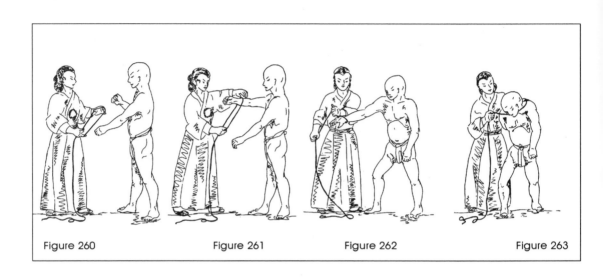

Figure 260 Figure 261 Figure 262 Figure 263

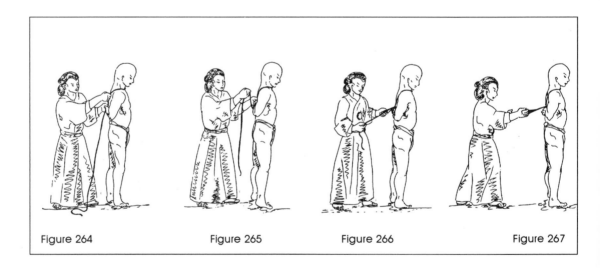

Figure 264 Figure 265 Figure 266 Figure 267

restrict the prisoner's arms but not his hands, thereby allowing the prisoner to perform necessary functions such as eating and relieving himself. Other tying techniques permit the prisoner to use his legs to walk but not to run. Of course, still other tying techniques completely immobilize the prisoner. The most extreme techniques of hojo-jutsu can produce pain or, if the prisoner struggles violently to escape, even death.

TECHNIQUE NUMBER 1

This technique was primarily used in feudal days to move a prisoner quickly from one room to another. Once mastered, it should take no longer than four seconds to perform. Once you learn how to manipulate your subject and to keep him constantly off balance by pushing and pulling on the cord, you will understand how he expedites your performance. When a police officer demonstrated this technique on me, I realized without a shadow of a doubt that the harder I struggled the easier it became for him to secure me.

To start this technique, first obtain a nylon cord approximately 10 feet long and make a loop (not a slipknot) in one end, much as you would make a cowboy lasso. Place the looped end in your right hand and the opposite end on the outside of your left thumb and forefinger (Figure 260). I find a left-foot- and left-hand-forward posture best suits this technique. Place the excess rope to your right and behind you.

As the attacker reaches for or pushes you with his right hand, quickly slide your left foot forward and place the open end of the rope around his wrist (Figure 261). Immediately upon encircling the attacker's wrist (Figure 262), pull downward and to your right with your right hand, thereby tightening the loop on the attacker's wrist and forcing him to step across his body to his left with his right foot.

As shown in Figure 263, slide your feet to your left, with your left foot moving first. Bring the attacker's right arm behind his back and up toward his shoulder blades by seizing the rope at his wrist with your left hand. Bring your right hand over the attacker's head and loop the rope under his chin from left to right.

You should now be standing to the right rear of the attacker. Reaching with your left hand, take hold of the attacker's left wrist and bring it behind his back to where his wrists will meet (Figure 264). Starting on the outside of the attacker's left wrist (the side closer to your body), make three complete wraps with the cord. The loose end of the cord should be in your right hand but on top of your right index finger.

Reach with your left hand to the attacker's left shoulder blade (Figure 265). Slide the back of your left hand inside the cord across the attacker's back at shoulder-blade-level until you can slide your fingers under the opposite cord, which should be located at the attacker's right shoulder blade. Squeezing your fingers into a fist, take your right index finger with the cord looped over it and place it under the two existing cords until you have formed about a two-inch loop.

As in Figure 266, take hold of the inside of the loop with your left hand and firmly slide everything down toward the attacker's wrist. Now pull the rope with your right hand, making the loop smaller and tighter, but leave the index and second finger of your left hand inside the loop. Reach under the cord (which is secured in your right hand) and pull it with the second finger of your left hand to create a new loop in your left hand. When this is completed, pull straight toward the floor, thereby making the connection tight. Continue making these loops—which resemble a crocheted chain stitch—until you come to the end of the cord.

Figure 267 shows the conclusion of the technique.

TECHNIQUE NUMBER 2

This technique is actually a prisoner-restraining technique. It immobilizes the arms but leaves the hands free for eating and so forth.

The technique starts as in Figure 260. Then place the loop over the prisoner's right forearm just above the elbow (Figure 268). With your right hand pull the cord across his back and over his left shoulder. Reaching over his head, place the cord across his neck, under his chin, and back over his right shoulder, thereby forming an X between his shoulder blades (Figure 269).

As shown in Figure 270, take the cord in either hand and place it under his left bicep just above the elbow. [*Note:* If the prisoner becomes violent, give a hard pull with the end of the cord; the outcome will be most devastating.] Wrap the cord around his arm three times. You may find it necessary to move the cord from hand to hand while doing this. At

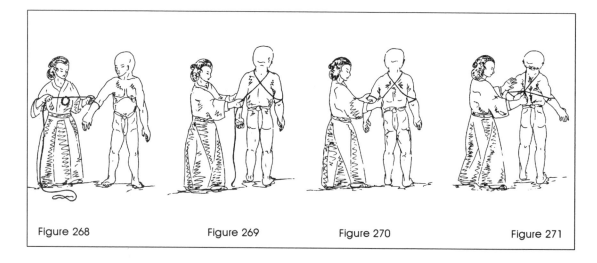

Figure 268   Figure 269   Figure 270   Figure 271

the conclusion of the three wraps, the loose end of the cord should be in your right hand, but on top of your right index finger. With your left hand, reach to the center of the prisoner's back where the X is formed and place your fingers under the X with your palm facing toward you. Put the end of the cord (which is on your right index finger) under the X and grasp it with your left hand. Then pull the cord through to form a loop, as in Technique Number 1. Keeping hold of the cord with both hands, pull straight down toward the prisoner's waist with both hands.

Now pull the cord with your right hand, making the loop smaller and tighter, but leave the index and second fingers of your left hand inside the loop (Figure 271). Reach under the cord (which is secured in your right hand) and pull it with the second finger of your left hand, thereby creating a new loop in your left hand. When this is completed, pull straight toward the floor, thereby making the connection tight. Continue making these loops—which resemble a crocheted chain stitch—until you come to the end of the cord.

The next two techniques are also part of the Itatsu Ryu. However, they are not considered hojo techniques, because they are not principally designed for tying; rather, they are considered self-defense methods using a rope. These days you'll find that a common belt will work wonderfully. In these figures, the defender is shown using a martial art obi folded in half, because when you practice these wazas, you will probably be in some type of martial art gi. Remember that an ordinary belt will be too short to fold in half.

Figure 272   Figure 273   Figure 274

TECHNIQUE NUMBER 3

Standing in a left-foot- and left-hand-forward posture, take the looped end of the belt in your left hand and stretch the belt tightly between both hands (Figure 272). The attacker holds the knife in his right hand, with his right foot to the rear.

In Figure 273, as the attacker steps forward with his right foot and thrusts downward, slide your left foot 45 degrees to your left followed by your right, simultaneously blocking the attacker's forearm with the center of the belt placed at a 45-degree angle. Whether the attacker steps forward with his right foot or simply slides forward with his left is not important; the results will be the same.

Slide straight forward with your left foot, followed by your right foot (Figure 274). Bring the belt horizontal and push it up and behind the attacker's head with a circular motion, capturing the attacking wrist in the process. The attacker's right forearm should be resting against his right earlobe.

Slide your right hand down the belt and across the attacker's body until your knuckles reach the attacker's right armpit (Figure 275). Give a severe pull downward with your left hand, thereby securing your right hand in the hollow of the armpit. Continue pulling with your left hand toward your left knee. The attacker will lose his balance to his

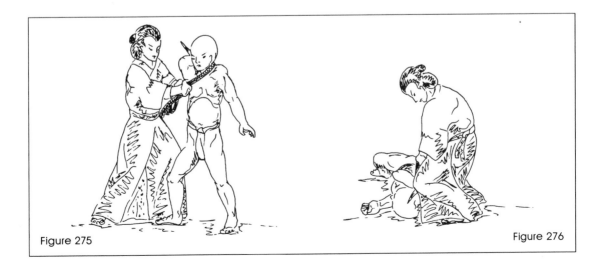

Figure 275   Figure 276

right side. Continue pulling with your left hand toward your left knee until the attacker starts to fall. (He will be falling counterclockwise.)

As his legs and hips touch the floor (Figure 276), start a slight upward motion with the belt. Now take a small step to the rear with your left foot. As the right side of the attacker's head reaches a point just below your left knee, slide your left foot forward so that you can kneel with your left knee on the attacker's right temple. Two things can happen at this point. One, you can simply pull straight up with both ends of the belt, thereby slowly forcing the attacker to drop the weapon. Or two, you can push violently down with your left knee while pulling simultaneously with both hands toward your chest and break his neck.

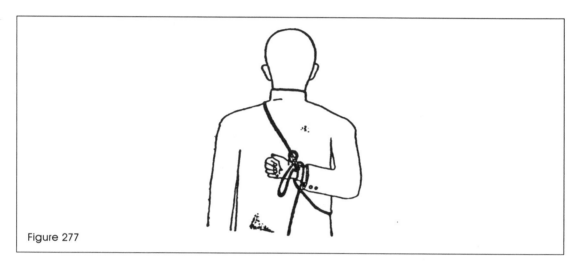

Figure 277

Figure 277 depicts another type of hojo tying. The details of the technique are not included, but I'll explain the significance of it below. [*Note:* I should mention that there are absolutely no knots in these techniques; therefore by simply pulling the loose end of the cord, the entire tying procedure will unravel except for the original loop. That loop has to be removed by you or the subject physically.] If you study Figure 277, you will notice the large loop on the outside of the person's wrist. Always available in each technique, this loop is called the "locking loop." Simply place the loop around the closer wrist and pull the loose end of the cord until the loop is tight, and the rope will not unravel. Keep in mind that the locking loop has to be physically unwrapped before an untying chain reaction will occur.

TECHNIQUE NUMBER 4

Take a defensive posture like that in the previous technique. The attacker holds the knife in his right hand and prepares to thrust it at your stomach (Figure 278). His right foot will be in the rear.

As the attacker steps and lunges forward with the knife (Figure 279), slide your left foot forward and to your left and bring your right heel in line with your left heel. Simultaneously, slide your left hand up and your right hand down toward the end of your belt and block the attacking arm with the center of the belt. The belt should be held at a 45-degree angle.

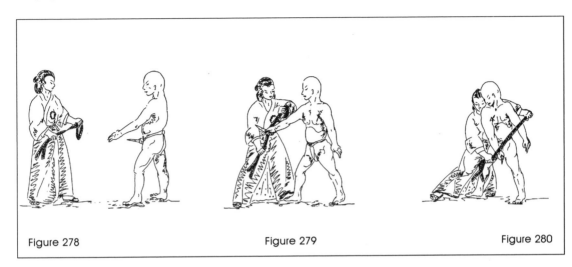

Figure 278

Figure 279

Figure 280

Upon contact with the attacker's forearm, push the belt away from you and downward, sliding your right hand up the belt until it reaches a point just above the attacker's head (Figure 280). Now make a circular motion with both hands, the left hand toward the attacker's left shoulder and the right hand toward his groin, keeping the belt stretched tightly.

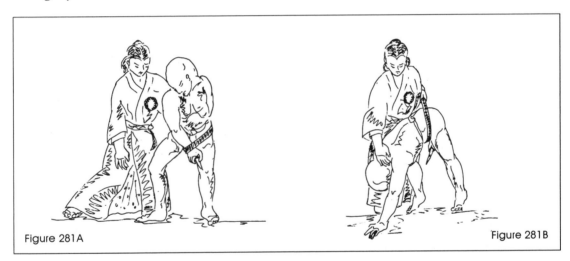

Figure 281A

Figure 281B

In Figure 281A, the attacker's right arm is now secured in the vicinity of his groin. Slide your right hand to the end of the belt encircling the attacker's hips until you can place the end of the belt in your left hand, then combine the two ends. It is important to keep the belt pulled as tightly as possible from this point forward. Reach with your right hand to the back of the attacker's neck, step forward with your right foot and force the attacker off balance forward (Figure 281B).

I think it very important to repeat the reminder that any technique is only as effective as the practitioner is proficient. The secret of jujitsu lies not in the technique itself but in the repetitious and boring practice of basics. For instance, take *kokyu nage* (breath throw) in Sensei Morihei Ueshiba's aikido. Once while I was practicing in Japan at one of the police dojos, an aikido master told me he had been O Sensei's uke for that particular technique for more than twenty years before O Sensei taught it to him. With this in mind, if you find the belt techniques complicated, my advice is to seek an instructor.

Figure 282

CHAPTER TEN
Yawari

YAWARI COMES from the word *yawara,* which is loosely translated as "jujitsu." As far as I can determine, the origin of the yawari has been lost in time; however, some sources believe that the yawari was invented by the ninja. If you refer back to the chapter concerning atemi waza, you can probably relate the use of these weapons to the jujitsu time chart.

The old yawari was approximately 6 inches long. The diameter of the shaft was about $1\frac{1}{8}$ inches in the middle, tapering down to $\frac{3}{4}$ of an inch. There was a $1\frac{1}{4}$-inch square at each end that tapered to a pyramid-shaped point (see Figure 282). The weapons were usually designed to be used in pairs, with one in each hand. We find this same weapon today modified and extensively carried, hanging from keychains, belt rings, purses, and even necklaces. The modern weapon is called *kubotan,* but it is nothing but the old yawari modified. If you practice with yawari, be extremely careful not to injure your partner by striking too hard. The yawari techniques are extremely painful if executed correctly and, in some cases, could cause permanent damage. Keep in mind the jujitsu time chart. As a great master once stated to his disciple, "Art is something that lies in the slender margin between the real and the unreal."

TECHNIQUE NUMBER 1

With tori in a left-foot- and left-hand-forward posture, uke reaches or strikes out with his right hand or fist (Figure 283).

In Figure 284, tori strikes upward and attacks the inside of uke's right wrist. Then, in Figure 285, tori immediately steps forward with his right foot and strikes the hollow of uke's left collarbone with his right hand. Uke's reaction will immediately be downward.

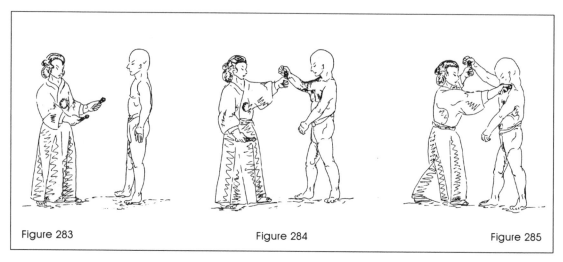

Figure 283

Figure 284

Figure 285

TECHNIQUE NUMBER 2

With tori in a left-hand- and left-foot-forward posture, uke steps forward with his right foot and reaches or strikes out with his hand or fist (Figure 286). Tori immediately strikes uke's middle forearm nerve with the point of his left yawari.

As uke withdraws his right arm, tori steps forward with his right foot at a 45-degree angle to his left foot, placing his right arm under uke's right elbow and the edge of his right yawari against the top inside part of his elbow (Figure 287). [*Note:* To find the correct spot when practicing, first locate the nerve with your finger.]

In Figure 288, tori pushes with his left hand downward while pulling toward himself with his right hand, thereby breaking uke's balance backward. Tori immediately steps forward with his left foot in the same direction he is facing (Figure 289). Tori withdraws his right hand and strikes downward into uke's solar plexus.

TECHNIQUE NUMBER 3

With tori in a right-hand- and right-foot-forward posture, uke strikes out with his right hand. Tori slides forward with his right foot to uke's center and strikes with the point of his left yawari just beneath the right side of uke's jaw. Uke will lean back either from pain or to avoid the attack. As he does so, tori immediately steps back with his left foot, places the bottom of his left yawari into the hollow of uke's right collarbone and pushes straight down. As uke loses his balance, tori kneels on his left knee and, with the inside point of his right yawari, strikes the inside of uke's right thigh approximately four inches from the groin (Figure 290).

TECHNIQUE NUMBER 4

With tori in a left-foot- and left-hand-forward posture, uke attacks with a right cross to tori's chin (Figure 291). Tori immediately slides forward with his left foot and strikes uke's right bicep with the outside point of tori's left yawari. As uke starts to withdraw his arm, tori immediately thrusts the inside point of his left yawari just below uke's left ear and jaw bone (Figure 292).

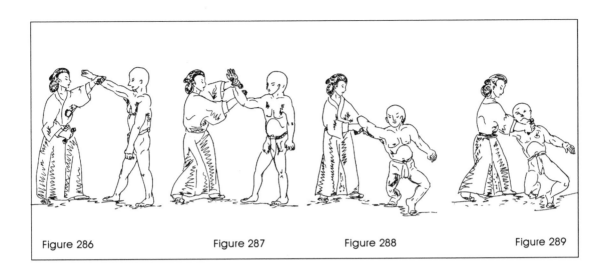

Figure 286   Figure 287   Figure 288   Figure 289

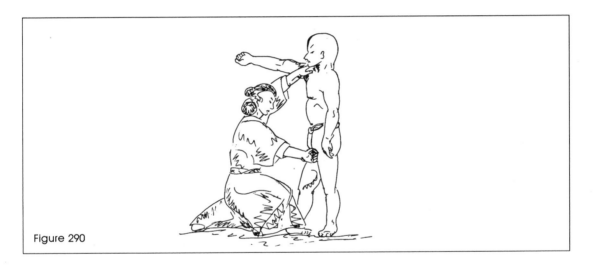

Figure 290

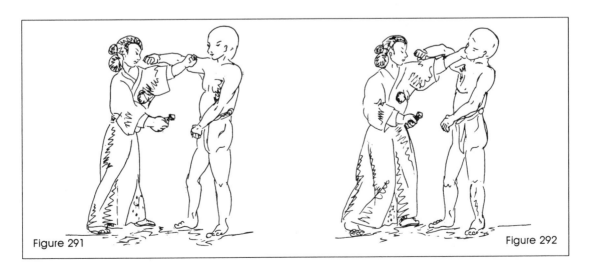

Figure 291   Figure 292

In Figure 293, tori immediately steps forward with his right foot to the center of uke's body and, with the inside point of his right yawari, strikes the opposite side of uke's jaw just below the right ear. Tori immediately turns the inside points of both yawaris upward alongside uke's ears and brings the outside points straight down into the hollows of uke's collarbones (Figure 294).

Figure 293

Figure 294

> **"When you do something, you should burn yourself completely, like a good bonfire, leaving no trace of yourself."**
>
> —Zen Saying

CHAPTER ELEVEN
Jo Jutsu

IT IS MY extreme pleasure to dedicate this final chapter to my sensei, Master Harutane Chiba, practitioner of the Hokushin Ito Ryu style of kendo for sixty-eight years. Since he was born in 1924, you may wonder how he could have studied this art for so long. I will explain this later, but first let me introduce you to the heads of the Chiba family over the past millennium:

Kayano Wasuke Tsunenari	Hayami Tozaemon Mitsutaka
Chikamatsu Kanroku Yukishige	Hazama Shinroku Mitsukaze
Sugaya Hannojo Masatoshi	Hara Soemon Mototoki
Horibe Yahyoe Kanemaru	Ohishi Kuranasuke Yoshitaka
Yato Uemoshichi Norikane	Kataoka Gengoemon Takafusa
Fuwa Kazuemon Masatane	Nakamura Kansuke Masatoki
Tsutane Chiba	Muramatsu Kihei Hidenao
Okuda Magodayu Shigemori	Kunitane Chiba
Ohishi Chikara Yoshikane	Uichi Chiba
Onodera Junai Hidekazu	Harutane Chiba
Isogai Jurozaemon Masahisa	Toshitane Chiba
Chiba Saburobei Mitsutada	

Quite an impressive list. It is customary only in the samurai tradition to take a new surname after death. This is the reason for all the different names in the above list.

Tsutane Chiba (1118–1212), the seventh generation in the Chiba family line, formed a style of fencing that became known as the Hokushin (North Star) way of kendo. This style became so famous that it was soon—and still is today—one of the three greatest styles of fencing in Japan and throughout the world. This style has transcended generations, becoming a legend in Japanese history. Samurai of old have faded in the yellow pages of books and time, but their spirit lives on throughout eternity in the art of kendo.

All samurai traits, such as discipline, respect, and honor, live on through this art. Through kendo, one can use the legacy left by the samurai to improve his or her daily living. Chiba Sensei once said, "The primary aim of kendo practice is to learn to be successful and victorious in life without drawing the sword. Achieve your goals honestly without violence or deceit. A no hands victory." One who learns the true way of the sword has truly learned something; he carries the moral values of kendo into his daily living, whether it be in the home, in the community, or on the job.

Sensei Harutane Chiba was born near the city of Nagasaki, Japan. Since he was the eldest son, it was his duty to carry on the style known as the Hokushin Chiba Kendo Ryu, which had been in existence for over 750 years. When he was only seven, he began learning the art under the tutelage of his highly skilled grandfather and father, Kunitane Chiba and Uichi Chiba, respectively. He became a master of kendo. Chiba Sensei was the thirty-sixth generation of the Chiba family. Desiring to spread the philosophy of kendo to all, Chiba Sensei opened a dojo in Osaka after the Second World War. The dojo's membership currently exceeds three hundred teachers and students ranging in age from five to seventy years. Girls and women practice there as well as boys and men. Having succeeded in Japan, Chiba Sensei had dreams of spreading his way of kendo to the United States, and this is where our paths were destined to cross.

A Japanese newspaper article about Mr. Chiba appeared on January 17, 1980 (see Figure 295). The translation given here is not verbatim but, rather, a summary of the important points. This article was printed in the *Sun Rise Newspaper,* which has the largest circulation in the world (the *New York Times* having the second largest). It is important to note that this was the first time since 1944 that this newspaper had published an article on any martial artist. The headline read, "Chiba Style Swordfighting Introduced to Texas Cowboys. Kendo Popularity Rising Rapidly in Cowboy Country." The article continued as follows:

> *Mr. Chiba, living in Osaka, Japan, is a 36th-generation samurai from the Chiba family. The Chiba clan was one of the most famous and influential samurai families in all of Japan. According to Chiba families' recorded documents, over 750 years ago Chiba's ancestors were very powerful warriors. Mr. Chiba's ancestors created a special Japanese sword fencing style known as the Hokushin style. After the war, all kendo was banned in Japan by General MacArthur, and there was a period of ten years when there was no Chiba style of kendo. During that time, Mr. Chiba opened a printing company. When the allies lifted the ban on martial arts, Chiba Sensei reopened his kendo school. Sensei Chiba's dream, even in those days, was to introduce the Chiba style of kendo to the United States and maybe someday all over the world.*
>
> *In 1978 Mr. Chiba was invited by the American Kendo Federation to come to Texas and officiate at the Southern United States Kendo Tournament, where he met Mr. Darrell Craig, president of the federation. After discussing with Mr. Craig his idea of bringing kendo, Chiba style, to the United States and learning that Mr. Craig needed a head instructor, plans were made for Mr. Chiba to become the Head Kendo Instructor at Mr. Craig's school.*
>
> *Mr. Chiba feels that kendo is good not only for physical development but, most important, for mental development. He has turned over his Japanese businesses to his sons and has begun learning English at the university. When Mr. Chiba visited the United States in 1976, he could not*

Figure 295

Figure 296

Figure 297

Figure 298

speak or understand English and had a very difficult time trying to demonstrate Chiba style of kendo, other than to American nesei (second-generation Japanese people). Mr. Chiba feels that kendo is not only technique but learning how to be a gentleman and a person with extreme pride within himself. He feels that it is a very self-disciplined martial art. The kendo man learns etiquette, a sense of justice, courage, and a quick reflex. These qualities can be applied in daily life at the office or at home. As Mr. Chiba had enjoyed John Wayne movies, meeting Mr. Craig was the perfect opportunity for him to see the West and meet cowboys. Mr. Chiba's feelings are that the cowboys of old had the same spirit as the samurai of Japan. Chiba Sensei can tell through his visits to the United States that kendo's popularity is growing with great speed.

The Chiba mark, or family crest, is a circle with a dot at the top (see Figure 296). The circle represents the universe, and the dot, which is the Japanese way to make a star, represents the north star, therefore indicating the Hokushin Ito Ryu (North Star Style of the Sword): the north star never moves, and everything in the universe must move around it. Figure 297 shows the front cover of the 1978 *All Japan Kendo Monthly Magazine*. If you look at Sensei Chiba's ancestor, you will note the tremendous resemblance that has endured through the centuries in the Chiba family. Figure 298 shows the scrolls indicating how the Hokushin Ito Ryu Style was formatted from the stars. When I visited Sensei in Japan, I had the opportunity to look through literally box after box of these fascinating scrolls.

I have met many men whom I have respected; others I have envied. But none have I loved like Chiba Sensei. Not only was he my guiding star, but he consumed my martial life. Anyone who met this man found something mysterious about his manners. His very presence made everyone aware that something outstanding was about to happen. He never asked for anything. He expected nothing in return for his vast library of knowledge. But if you were willing to learn, he would spend hours explaining the smallest detail of a tedious technique. He never became frustrated and he never moved on until he was sure you were completely satisfied with the results.

I know he is missed by many and will never be forgotten by those he touched. So, I leave you with a thought from Rudyard Kipling:

> *So I'll meet 'im later on*
> *at the place where 'e has gone—*
> *Where it's always double drill and no canteen.*

Several of the following jo techniques against the sword were taught to me by Sensei Chiba. I hope you enjoy learning, not only from the present, but in this case most definitely from Japan's past.

* * *

The length and diameter of the Japanese jo are approximately 50 inches and 1 inch, respectively. It can be round or hexagonal in shape, depending on your preference. It is normally made of white oak. If cost is not a factor, you may purchase one in a harder wood, such as ironwood, which has a darker or almost black color. The oak used in making the jo has a high water content, which gives it stability and weight. The very close grain prevents splintering as it slides through your hands. I feel there are very few acceptable substitutes for Japanese oak. Some years ago, I had several jos made from purple heart. It was a very costly but suitable endeavor. I recommend purchasing one already made because there are few substitutes that meet the correct requirements. Beware of jos or bos made from soft woods like pine; they break easily and become extremely dangerous to you and your partner. In practicing the techniques against a sword, a wooden boken without a sword guard will suffice for the sword.

In fighting or defending with the stick—whether it be 3 feet (sometimes referred as a *hanbo*), 4 feet (*jo*), or 6 feet (*bo*)—the majority of the techniques are the same. I think the hanbo and *jutte*, which was a police type of iron trenching tool (also known as *junte*), were very similar in use, whereas the six-foot bo was considered more of a peasant's weapon. The true samurai naturally was familiar with all the weapons of that time.

The jo was originally introduced into Japanese martial history in the 1600s. Aikido practitioners will generally tell you the following story to explain how it came into being. According to the story, a samurai named Gonnosuke Muso invented the art of jo jutsu after being beaten in a duel with the great Musashi Miyamoto. The story goes that Musashi, after getting the upper hand in the duel, let Muso live.

I am not a Japanese historian by any means, but among the thousands of articles written about Musashi, the aikido version of the fight seems to be the only time Musashi let anyone live after an encounter. Whether that outcome is true or not, Gonnosuke Muso is credited with developing the majority of the jo techniques we know today.

The story continues with Gonnosuke Muso retreating into the mountains, where he meditated for several years. Through this meditation, he was given a divine insight which led him to develop a style of jo jutsu he called Shindo-Muso Ryu. Supposedly, he then challenged Musashi Miyamoto to another duel, and this duel resulted in his sparing Musashi's life. Here again, I find it hard to believe that anyone would have spared the great swordmaster's life. To have killed such a famous samurai as Musashi—who had 68 recorded duels to the death—would have brought the victor more fame and wealth than he could imagine. In any case, you should do your own research on both masters.

The Shindo-Muso Ryu jo jutsu still exists. One of its practitioners, with whom many martial artists in the western hemisphere are familiar, was Donn F. Draeger. Sensei Draeger was a highly skilled judo practitioner who received the 6th grade black belt from the Kodokan, with a teaching license. I believe he was one of the very few—if not the only—Anglo-Saxon to achieve this rank. Sensei Draeger, who died in 1982, was the author of numerous authoritative books about martial arts that are recommended reading if you desire to further your knowledge of the jo.

During the time that Sensei Draeger was active in this style, the head master of Shindo-Muso Ryu jo jutsu was Sensei Shimizu Takaji. Through Mr. Kobayashi, Sensei of the Imperial Police, I had the opportunity to meet Sensei Takaji in 1973 at the Tokyo Budokan. Sensei Takaji had been conducting a jodo class in the basement of the Budokan where martial arts are taught in the evenings. His manipulation of the jo was absolutely outstanding. Sensei Takaji passed away shortly thereafter. There was some confusion as to who would succeed him as head master, so Sensei Draeger sought another style in which to train. About this time, Sensei Draeger evidently met Sensei Risuke Otake of the Tenshin Shoden Katori Shinto Ryu, about which he coauthored a book. This five-hundred-year-old style of swordsmanship, like many old styles, had bojutsu interwoven in its arsenal. I am sure this intrigued Sensei Draeger and led him to continue his jo practices.

All of this discussion leads to one important point: jodo is an independent martial art. It is governed by the All Japan Jodo Federation, although it comes under the overall control of the All Japan Kendo Federation. There are still several independent small jo jutsu styles in Japan. Some belong to the Federation and some do not, depending on the way they rank their students. Small independent dojos are virtually impossible to gain entry into without a proper introduction and sponsor. Set forth below are the ranks and teaching licenses for Japanese budo that are normally awarded on the basis of scheduled examinations in Japan throughout the year. *Yodan* examinations and below are given at local prefectures, while *godan* examinations and above are given yearly at a national level. Teaching licenses are also awarded at the yearly examination. The following information may be used as a guide for rank requirements.

Grades and Requirements

nidan	one year after the candidate has passed an examination for shodan
sandan	two years after the candidate has passed an examination for nidan
yodan	two years after the candidate has passed an examination for sandan
godan	three years after the candidate has passed an examination for yodan
rokudan	four years after the candidate has passed an examination for godan
shichidan	five years after the candidate has passed an examination for rokudan
hachidan	eight years after the candidate has passed an examination for shichidan

Teaching Licenses

renshi	three years after passing an examination for godan
kyoshi	seven years after passing an examination for renshi; the candidate must be a minimum of thirty-one years old.
hanshi	twenty years after passing an examination for kyoshi; the candidate must be a minimum of fifty-five years old.

These time requirements should provide some useful basis on which to judge any instructor claiming high rank and teaching license.

The chances of finding an instructor with a license of renshi, kyoshi, or hanshi are relatively scarce, even in Japan. Any claim to possess such a license made by any martial artist should be very carefully investigated before deciding to train under him. High black belt grades—especially by youthful "senseis"—should always be viewed with great suspicion. If you wish to verify the legitimacy of any "sensei" claiming such a remarkable credential, you may write to the following address:

Kobudo Shinkokai
5-3 Kojimachi
Chiyoda-ku
Tokyo 102, Japan

Try to make your inquiry in Japanese first. This may be accomplished by contacting your nearest Japanese Consulate and requesting its assistance. Keep in mind that this pertains only to an art ruled by one of the Japanese do federations. In a particular ryu or old school, you would have to get in touch with the *hombu dojo* (the main dojo). Do not expect a lengthy or quick response.

It is not my intention to show a particular jodo or jo jutsu system in this book, but to introduce some jo stick techniques that are taught widely in Japan to law enforcement personnel. I will cover posture and ready stances, apprehending techniques, jo versus the sword, and kata.

Before we start, a note of interest: Hata Sensei stated to me that he had never seen a left-handed Japanese sensei of any kind. I remember him smiling and saying, "That doesn't mean there aren't any, just that in my fifty-six years of learning and traveling throughout Japan, I had never seen a left-handed sensei until I came to the United States." In Japan, when these techniques were being readily used, all men of upper-class status were right-handed. Sensei Hata's notes reflected only right-hand attacks; my notes also reflect only right-hand attacks. All I can say to left-handed people is this: you'll have to continue doing what you've always done in the past. Simply do it upside down or backward!

Figure 299

Figure 300

Figure 301

Figure 302

Figure 303

Figure 304

KEISATSO JO JUTSU

KAMAI (Posture)

Figure 299 shows *shizentai*, natural standing posture. Figure 300 shows *chudan-no-kamai*, the basis of all five postures and considered the most effective. This posture permits variation for attack and defense with each movement of the opponent. The right foot is forward, while the left hand is about one fist's width from the abdomen; the right hand is about two fists' length in front of the left hand. The end of the jo will be pointing at the opponent's throat.

In Figure 301, *gedan-no-kamai* is accomplished when you lower one end of the jo. The end of the jo should be at the level of the opponent's knees. Make sure your head is up and looking straight across at your opponent's eyes. When looking at your opponent, see him as you would a picture on the wall. You focus on the picture, yet your vision takes in the entire wall. With this concept in mind, his eyes become the picture and his body, the wall.

For *migi-hassou-no-kamai* (Figure 302) step back with your right foot and bring both hands to the right side of the body. Your right hand will be about even with your chin, and your left hand will be even with your solar plexus.

To achieve *migi-jodan-no-kamai* (Figure 303) bring your left foot forward. At the same time, raise your hands in a circular motion to the front and over your head, stopping with the left hand just above your eye level.

For *waki-no-kamai* (Figure 304) starting in the chudan-no-kamai, bring your right foot to the rear and, without changing your grip, simultaneously bring both hands to your lower right side. The jo should be pointing downward and to the rear.

The next two figures are related to a particular ryu or style.

In Figure 305, *jodo-chudan-no-kamai,* there are two basic hand positions when using the jo: the *ken-te* (sword hand), as seen in the chudan-no-kamai (Figure 300), and the other, which I'll call *jo-te* (wood hand), as seen in Figure 305. In using the jo-te, the thumb of the forward hand, whether it be the right or left, will be toward you, and your elbows will be bent about 10 degrees outward.

For *jodo-jodan-no-kamai* (Figure 306) from the jodo-chudan-no-kamai, push outward with your rear hand in an upward circular motion, stopping your forward hand approximately at your hairline. Your rear hand is just above eye level. This kamai can be accomplished by stepping forward with your right foot as you simultaneously raise your jo.

Figure 305　　　　　　　　　　　　　　　　　　　　　　　　　Figure 306

APPREHENDING TECHNIQUES

SIDE CIRCLE THROW *(Jo Tebuki Gaeshi Toko Tomoe Nage)*

Standing in shizentai, and with the jo in your right hand, start your technique by stepping forward with your right foot. Using your right wrist, snap the lower end of the jo upward into the attacker's groin (Figure 307). [*Note:* Be sure you are close enough to your attacker to strike his groin without moving your right hand position on the jo.] The normal reaction to this attack is for the attacker to bend forward at the hips and grab the jo with his hand, thumb down. Generally (and you can assure this by directing the jo slightly to his right) the attacker will grab the jo with his right hand.

As the attacker grabs the jo with his right hand, pull back and downward by sliding your rear foot and then your front foot a half step to the rear. Maintain correct posture; do not bend over. As in Figure 308, reach forward with your left hand and grasp the back of the attacker's right hand, placing your left thumb on the attacker's right thumb. Keeping your right foot in place, rotate the top four or five inches of the jo to the inside of and over the attacker's wrist (counterclockwise), using your left thumb to press the jo firmly against the attacker's right wrist joint.

Stepping straight forward with your right foot, press down with your left thumb and pull slightly forward and down at a 45-degree angle to your left. This will break the attacker's balance off his right little toe (Figure 309). Pivot on the ball of your right foot, moving the heel 90 degrees to your right. Continue to rotate your body by moving your left foot around behind the right foot (see Photograph 14). Your right knee will be slightly bent.

As in Figure 310, keeping the attacker's momentum forward and to his right, drop to your left knee quickly and place the jo between his legs and against his left thigh. [*Note:* You may also strike the attacker in the groin with the jo.]

Figure 311 shows the execution of the throw *tomoe nage*. The off-balance will remain at a right 45-degree angle. Push forward and down with your left thumb on top of the jo against the attacker's wrist bone. Simultaneously pull toward yourself and upward with your right hand. The attacker should do a somersault roll 20 degrees off his right little toe. This technique will conclude with the jo in a vertical position.

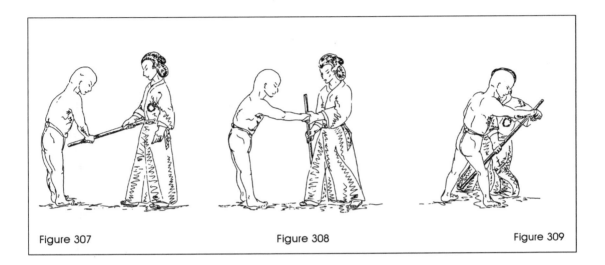

Figure 307   Figure 308   Figure 309

Figure 310   Figure 311

ROLLING OVER THE WRIST WITH A STICK *(Kote Mawashi With The Jo)*

This waza starts in a left-foot- and left-hand-forward posture. The end of your jo will be pointing at the attacker's solar plexus—that is, at a slight 20-degree angle upward (Figure 312).

As shown in Figure 313, step forward with your left foot, follow with your right foot, and thrust (*tsuki*) with the jo, keeping in line with the attacker's solar plexus. Keep your weight distributed evenly on the balls of both feet and maintain correct posture. The attacker will grab the jo with his right hand, thumb across the top of the jo, and step back with his left foot, as if to push the jo away or jerk it from your hands.

Pull slightly by sliding your right foot and then your left to the rear. Simultaneously rotate the jo to the outside with an upward clockwise motion (Figure 314).

As in Figure 315, slide forward with your left foot, followed by your right, simultaneously grasping the attacker's right thumb and forefinger with your left thumb and forefinger. Make sure the end of your jo is now pointing directly between the attacker's eyes. Using both hands, push the jo forward so that the attacker's right arm makes a 90-degree angle at the elbow. Now, with a quick snap of the wrist, press forward and down, simultaneously sliding your feet forward. As the attacker falls backward, release the grip on his hand so that he may execute his off-balance without injury. (*Caution!* Do this waza gently or you may break your opponent's wrist immediately with your snapping wrist movement!)

STICK MAJOR RIGHT SIDE BLOW—FOREARM ARMLOCK *(Jo O-Migi-Ate Ude-Hishigi)*

This waza starts with the jo in the hidari gedan-no-kamai (left low posture) Figure 316. The attacker is in a left forward posture.

The attacker steps forward with his right foot and reaches with his right hand. For practical purposes the attacker is unarmed, but this waza could be used against an armed attacker. (Keep in mind that this is a Japanese police restraining technique.) As in Figure 317, step back with your right foot while rotating the jo clockwise and strike the attacker's right kidney.

Move your left foot back and to your left about a half step and your right foot forward a half step so that your feet are parallel. [*Note:* If your attacker is standing at twelve o'clock, your left and right feet will be at nine and three o'clock, respectively.] Now strike the attacker's left kidney (Figure 318).

Reverse your left-hand jo position, so that the left thumb is up. With your right hand, grab the attacker's right wrist, as in Figure 319. Place the jo on the back underside of the attacker's elbow and the far end of the jo between the attacker's legs.

Break the attacker's balance by pushing forward and down with the jo on his elbow (Figure 320). Step forward with your left foot and continue pushing down with the jo. The jo may slide to the attacker's armpit as you are stepping forward. [*Note:* This waza can be carried to a further conclusion by simply stepping forward with your right foot and kneeling on your left knee. This will pin the attacker to the ground.] Again, caution is advised with regard to the amount of pressure you apply to your partner's elbow.

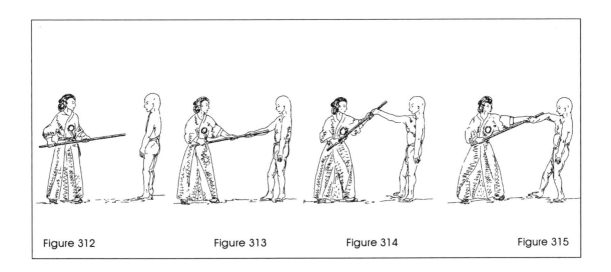

Figure 312   Figure 313   Figure 314   Figure 315

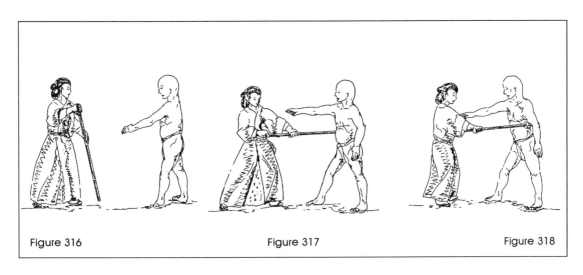

Figure 316   Figure 317   Figure 318

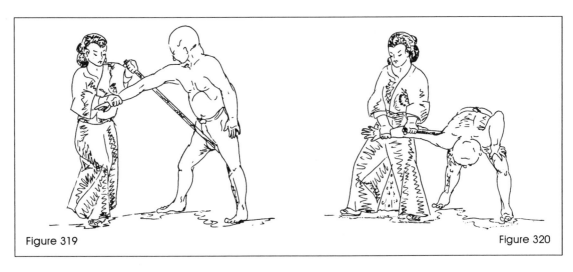

Figure 319   Figure 320

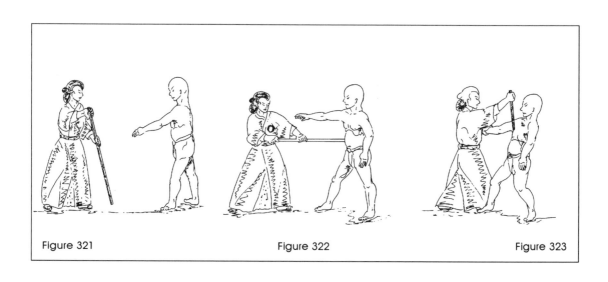

Figure 321   Figure 322   Figure 323

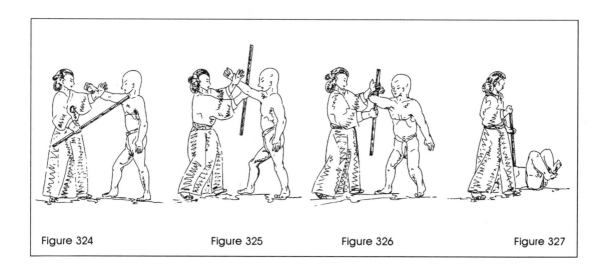

Figure 324   Figure 325   Figure 326   Figure 327

SIDE REAR DROP *(Jo O-Migi-Ate—Yoko-Ura-Otoshi)*

Figures 321 and 322 are exactly the same as Figures 316 and 317 in the previous waza.

After you have finished your strike in Figure 322, rotate your right hand so that your palm is facing upward on the jo. Reach with your left hand and seize the attacker's right wrist (Figure 323). (Your left palm will be away from you.) Place the jo behind the attacker's right side—preferably in the center of his buttocks and under his right armpit—by pushing upward with your right hand. Simultaneously, step with your right foot forward and to the outside of the attacker's front leg. Once the jo is in place, give a violent snapping motion with your right hand against the attacker's shoulder and to his rear. [*Note:* If the attacker is at twelve o'clock, your snapping motion will be applied at eleven o'clock.] The attacker's balance will be broken off his right little toe and to his rear. Once the attacker starts to fall backward, you have two options. First, you may leave the jo in place and quickly kneel. This will make the attacker fall across the jo, likely resulting in a dislocated rib. Second, you may withdraw the jo and let the attacker fall free.

STICK THRUST TO BENT ARM BAR
(Jo Tsuki-No-Ude Garami)

This waza begins with you in gedan-no-kamai—that is, the jo is in your right hand. The far end of the jo is approximately one inch off the floor; the other end is behind your right elbow. The jo is in a naturally held position at approximately 45 degrees. Your grip will be about one-third down from the top end. Your feet will be about shoulder width apart and parallel with each other. As the attacker strikes with his right hand, step forward with your left foot. It makes no difference whether the attacker steps with his right foot or slides forward with his left foot. As shown in Figure 324, block his attacking right hand with the back of your left hand. Simultaneously squeeze the jo with your right hand, thereby bringing its far end to the center of the attacker's body, and thrust it forward to his throat. This movement can be done by snapping your right wrist upward while pushing forward with your right arm so that the jo travels at a 45-degree angle.

The attacker's balance will be broken straight backward. Just as the attacker begins to take a step backward, slide the attacking end of the jo under his right arm at the elbow, keeping your left hand in position at his wrist (Figure 325).

Reach for the jo with your left hand, keeping a small amount of pressure against the attacker's forearm. Push the attacker's forearm toward the jo and grasp the jo just above the attacker's elbow (Figure 326). Slide your left hand downward while simultaneously sliding your right hand upward on the jo, pinning the attacker's elbow in a 90-degree angle.

At this point, the attacker's balance will be off his right little toe. Once you have secured your grip, pull with both hands toward you so that the attacker's elbow is pointing at your chest. Now quickly pull up and counterclockwise until the attacker starts to fall to his right side. You may release your left hand grip at this time and allow the attacker to fall freely (Figure 327). (If you do not release your grip, but rather give a quick snapping motion with your right hand, it is possible to dislocate the attacker's elbow.) After the attacker has fallen backward and the jo has become free, you may thrust it into his solar plexus simply by sliding the jo through your left hand.

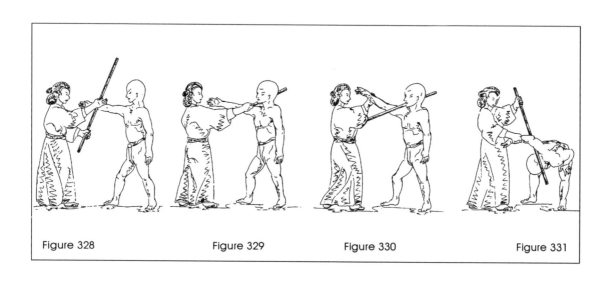

Figure 328   Figure 329   Figure 330   Figure 331

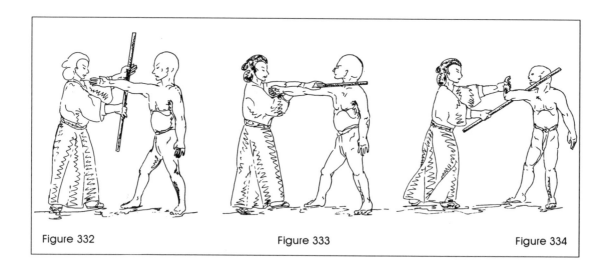

Figure 332   Figure 333   Figure 334

STRIKE TO THE SIDE OF THE HEAD
(Jo-Yoko-Men-Gyaku)

This waza starts with you standing in shizen hontai and then stepping into a right-forward stance. As the attacker reaches for you or attempts to strike you with his right hand, swing the bottom of the jo upward and to the inside of the attacker's forearm (Figure 328). Taking hold of the bottom of the jo (which previously was the top) with your left hand, step forward with your right foot.

As shown in Figure 329, strike the right side of the attacker's head just above the ear with the top inside of the jo. This is done by snapping the wrist and stepping forward slightly with the right foot.

Let the jo slide down the side of the attacker's neck until it rests on his shoulder. Release your right hand from the jo and seize the attacker's right wrist. Do this by reaching under the attacker's wrist with the back of your hand and turning your hand clockwise so that your fingers are pointing to your right (Figure 330).

Push upward with your left hand, keeping a firm grip on the attacker's wrist with your right hand. The off-balance will be to the attacker's left little toe—that is, 45 degrees to his left front (Figure 331). At this point you have two options. First, you may use it to restrain the attacker in this position, to await a police officer, or to move him to a desired location. Second, you may step forward with your left foot, keeping pressure on the back of the attacker's neck with the jo in your left hand. This will cause him to flip over on his back. If you do use the nage waza, be sure to withdraw the jo.

STRIKING THE SIDE OF THE NECK WITH BENT
ARM BAR *(Jo-Yoko-Ate-Hiji-Ude-Garami)*

This waza starts like Yoko-Men-Gyaku but, instead of striking the inside of the attacker's forearm, you strike with considerable force the attacker's right elbow, simultaneously stepping forward into a left forward stance (Figure 332). Kuzushi will be hidari maesumi-no-kuzushi. (If the attacker is using his left hand instead of his right, all movements are simply reversed.)

Upon contact with the attacker's elbow, immediately strike the left side of his head with the top end of the jo (Figure 333). This is done by pulling with your right hand and placing your right hand and the jo under your left armpit, while pushing with your left hand. Let the jo slide down the attacker's neck and rest on his left shoulder.

Reach with your left hand (palm facing in) to your right and place your left hand on the attacker's right wrist. Turning the attacker's palm to his face, bend his elbow to a 90-degree angle to your left (Figure 334). Step back with your right foot, bringing your right hand across your chest to your right. When the end of the jo in your right hand is even with your right side, push up with your right hand to a 45-degree angle. You may need to step forward with your right foot, depending on the position of the attacker. With a quick snap of your right wrist upward, you can bring the attacker crashing to the ground. By not releasing the attacker's wrist, you can also break his elbow.

LOCKING THE WRIST, STRIKING THE HEAD
(*Jo-Yoko-Ude-Gaeshi-Shomen*)

Taking the hidari shizentai, jo in the right hand, as the attacker reaches for you, slide your left foot forward about six inches, followed by your right foot. As shown in Figure 335, bring the bottom end of the jo up and to the outside of the attacker's right leg or hip.

Pass the jo over the top of the attacker's arm. Immediately reach with your left hand (palm facing in), thereby making an X with your forearms, and control the attacker's arm (Figure 336).

Lay the jo across the attacker's wrist and take hold of the jo with your left hand (Figure 337). With both of your hands, keep pressure against the sides of the attacker's wrist. At this point, your right-hand palm should be facing up, your left-hand palm facing down. [*Note:* When placing the jo around the attacker's wrist, try to keep the attacker's thumb pointing up.] This can be accomplished simply by keeping pressure inwardly with your hands on the jo, which will cause the jo to press on his wristbone, quite painfully. You may have to move your feet, depending on the amount of resistance by the attacker. If he attempts to grab your scrotum with his free hand, simply release one of your hands and the jo will strike him in the face. Then quickly follow up with Figure 340.

Keeping this tight grip, bend your elbows by pulling down and slightly upward. Kuzushi will be *mamae-no-kamai*. The attacker will fall to one or both knees (Figure 338).

Once the attacker is in a kneeling position (Figure 339), twist your hands counter-clockwise and release your top hand.

The attacker will fall backward and to his right side (Figure 340). Immediately raise the jo to jodan-no-kamai, step forward with your right foot and strike a blow to the attacker's head.

JO KORYU KATA

I would like to introduce the kata section of this chapter by quoting from "*Born for the Mat: A Kodokan Kata Textbook for Women Judo*," by Keiko Fukuda (5th ed. 1973):[1]

The Significance of Kata

Kata is made to study the basic movements of offense and defense in prearranged situations. Through the study of Kata, one will experience the true spirit of actual fighting and comprehend the principles of technique.

Key Points to Bear in Mind When Studying Kata

To learn correct ways of offense and defense, you must realize the importance of "Distance" and "Zanshin" (your remaining posture or position after execution). When one begins to practice Kata, the movements will be angular, due to the concentration involved in studying the prescribed methods; however, they will become smoother as you become better skilled, and your response to change will become natural movement upon opportunity.

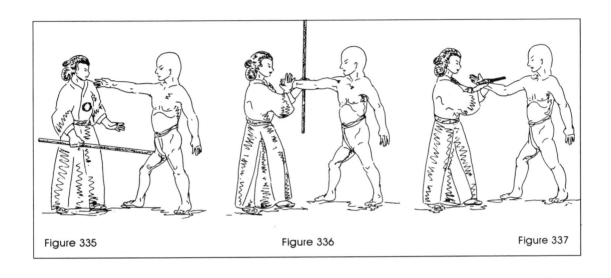

Figure 335   Figure 336   Figure 337

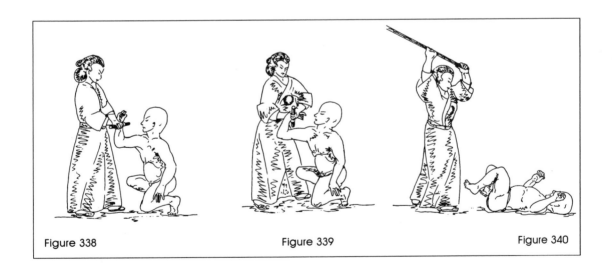

Figure 338   Figure 339   Figure 340

The firm and balanced movements, the correct ways in keeping eyes
upon the point, and refined composure will only be attained through long
and diligent practice.

Sensei Fukuda is the most remarkable and probably the most informed person about kata I have ever had the pleasure to meet and practice with. Several years ago, we invited Sensei Fukuda to my dojo for a kata clinic. Her teaching was astronomical for a young lady of seventy-eight years, particularly considering she had had heart surgery just four months prior to the clinic. I saw her demonstrate the throw *kata guruma* (of the judo *Nage-no-Kata* series) on one of my students with such precise accuracy that the student hardly realized he had passed completely over Sensei's head. It is also worthy to note that Sensei Fukuda is among the very few who actually took advice and personal instruction from the great Dr. Jigaro Kano, the founder of judo.

Kata is a system of prearranged exercises in attack and defense. There are literally thousands of different types of kata. We find kata in every traditional Japanese martial art. There are thirteen techniques that make up the kata in this jo system, but—in the interest of time and space—I will familiarize you with only the first six. Each technique in the kata can be applied from either side, but as a rule, when publicly demonstrating, the tori confines himself to applying them from the right posture—that is, migi shizentai or *migi jigotai*.

The katas illustrated in the following pages should be executed with a *bokuto*, or wooden sword, without a *tsuba*, or sword guard. The bokuto, which is sometimes referred to by its modern name, *boken* (*bo*—wood, *ken*—sword), should be made from a hard wood. White Japanese oak is very popular. Most of the bokens you find in the United States are of Taiwanese redwood; their construction is more rounded than the Japanese katana, which has a definite *shinogi* (ridges on the side of the blade). The shinogi is important for blocking. A good boken should have fine grain and no knots, and it should be balanced at a place that facilitates easy use. This is generally about two-thirds of the way from the tip.

JO KATA

KATA 1: Gedan Hiza Tsuki

When practicing the attack and defense of this kata, you and your partner must try to blend into perfect synchronization. You should look at your partner's eyes but see the entire body as if looking at your own reflection in a mirror. You should even concentrate on breathing together.

The kata starts with the participants facing each other, nine normal steps apart, the *uchidachi* (attacker) with the boken and the *shidachi* (defender) with the jo. Shidachi will hold the jo along the right side of his body, with the front of his hand facing out. The jo is thus behind his right forearm. The top of the jo should be even with shidachi's right shoulder. Uchidachi will have the boken on his left side, cutting edge up. His left hand is just below the handle, resting on his left hip or midthigh. Each person bows to the other from the waist, keeping his head straight so he can continually look into his opponent's eyes. Each person then takes three steps forward, starting with his right foot. (Figure 341 is the best example of proper foot position. Make sure that your feet are in these

Figure 341

Figure 342

positions.) Raise the heel of the left foot about $1^1/2$ to 2 inches off the floor. Raise the heel of the right foot just enough to slide a piece of paper under it.

On the third step, which will be with the right foot, shidachi brings the jo to jodo-chudan-no-kamai. Uchidachi will reach across his body with his right hand and pull the boken from his left hand. He should have the feeling of taking a sword out of the scabbard with the cutting edge up. Uchidachi then comes to chudan-no-kamai but, instead of having the jo in his hands, he will have the boken. Each weapon is held one fist away from the stomach, with the left hand about navel-high and the tip of each weapon pointing at the center of the opponent's neck. Do not stretch or tense your shoulders or arms; they must remain completely relaxed.

As shown in Figure 342, Shidachi squats on the balls of his feet with his heels off of the ground, his knees at a 90-degree angle right. His hand position is jodo-chudan-no-kamai. Uchidachi kneels on his left knee.

Keeping eye contact, each person rises to his feet, shidachi stepping forward with his right foot, uchidachi stepping back with his left foot (Figure 343).

In Figure 344, Shidachi then takes gedan-no-kamai, while uchidachi holds chudan-no-kamai. Each person takes five normal steps backward starting with the rear foot. They

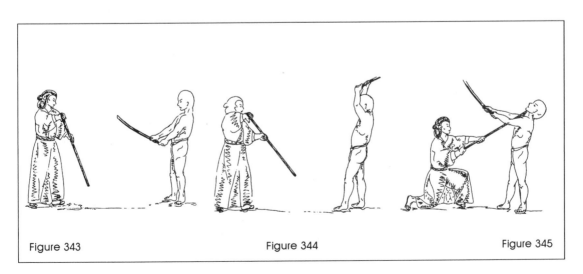

Figure 343

Figure 344

Figure 345

will now be nine steps apart. Uchidachi moves his left foot forward and assumes jodan-no-kamai. Shidachi slides his left foot forward, keeping gedan-no-kamai. His jo points at about uchidachi's knee level.

Each person takes three steps forward, starting with the front foot. Upon completion of the three steps, uchidachi and shidachi stop. Uchidachi will have his left foot forward; shidachi will have his right foot forward. Looking into the eyes, uchidachi senses an opening to cut shidachi's head. He steps forward with his right foot and starts his downward cut. Shidachi slides quickly forward with his left forward foot, rotating his right hand clockwise, coming to chudan-no-kamai; in a kneeling position, he attacks uchidachi's throat, pushing forward and up with the jo (Figure 345).

Uchidachi now slides his left foot one step backward; shidachi releases his attack and slides his right foot back while starting up. Each person assumes chudan-no-kamai and takes five small steps back, starting with the rear foot. This ends the first technique. [*Note:* Maintaining the proper *mawai* in these or any attacks is vital to the success of any waza.]

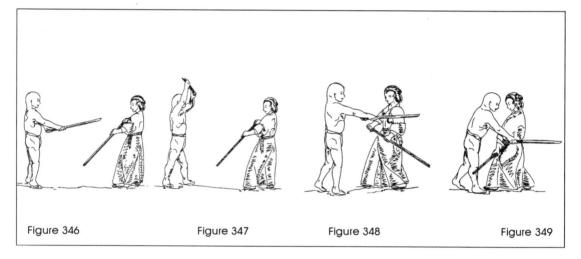

Figure 346   Figure 347   Figure 348   Figure 349

KATA 2: Jodo Yoko Hiza Guruma

This kata starts the same as Gedan Hiza Tsuki—that is, nine steps apart, followed by three forward steps beginning with the front foot. Uchidachi will stay in chudan-no-kamai and shidachi in gedan-no-kamai.

After taking the three steps forward to reach the proper distance, shidachi will have his left foot and hand forward; uchidachi will have his right foot and hand forward as shown in Figure 346.

Uchidachi, sensing a weak posture in shidachi's kamai, will immediately step forward with his right foot and strike the center of shidachi's forehead (Figure 347).

Shidachi waits under the sword until the cut is in "void." [*Note:* "Void" occurs when the attacker's mind is waiting to make contact.] As in Figure 348, when this void appears, shidachi steps with his right foot at a 45-degree angle to his right forward, migi-maesumi-no-kuzushi (see Figure 8 in Chapter Two), bringing the jo to *hidari-waki-no-kamai.*

Shidachi now quickly steps forward with his right foot and attacks uchidachi's right knee (Figure 349). Shidachi steps forward with his left foot. The step should be far enough so that, at the completion of this waza and just before uchidachi falls forward, uchidachi and shidachi will be momentarily left shoulder to left shoulder.

Figure 350   Figure 351   Figure 352

KATA 3: Jo Chudan Harai Shomen

This kata also starts as did the previous two—that is, nine steps apart, followed by the three forward steps. In Figure 350, uchidachi assumes a left-forward stance, holding the katana in jodan-no-kamai. Shidachi assumes a right-forward stance, holding the jo in a ken manner in chudan-no-kamai.

Uchidachi senses an opening to strike shidachi's *shomen*. He quickly steps forward with his right rear foot and strikes shidachi. Shidachi waits for the katana to start its forward movement, then takes a 45-degree half step forward to his right (migi-maesumi-no-kuzushi) with his right foot (Figure 351). Pushing both arms forward and making a quick snap with his wrist, shidachi will strike the side of uchidachi's katana on the shinogi.

Letting half of shidachi's block become his attack, shidachi strikes uchidachi's shomen as shown in Figure 352.

[*Note:* Shidachi may need to adjust his feet forward or backward depending on how hard uchidachi attacks.]

KATA 4: Chudan Gaeshi Yoko Men

This waza starts with both parties in chudan-no-kamai. As in Figure 353, shidachi will take the left jodo kamai, left hand and foot forward.

As the jo and katana cross as in Figure 353, shidachi tries to push against the side of uchidachi's katana by pulling to the right with his right rear hand and coming to jodan-no-kamai. Uchidachi quickly steps back with his right foot and brings his sword to jodan-no-kamai (Figure 354).

As quickly as uchidachi steps backward into jodan-no-kamai, he steps forward again with his right foot and strikes shidachi's shomen (Figure 355). With his right foot, shidachi steps to his right into migi-maesumi-no-kuzushi, raising his right hand above his head and receiving the blow on the side of his jo.

Shidachi lets the sword slide down his jo and pivots his left foot counterclockwise on the same line as his right foot. He lets the jo come around to the center of his back and strikes uchidachi's *yoko men* (Figure 356). As shidachi's left foot hits the floor, his hands will be in *ken te*.

KATA 5: Gedan Suriga Sumi Migi Ni Kote Guruma

As shown in Figure 357, in this waza, uchidachi takes chudan-no-kamai and shidachi holds *hidari-gedan-shizentai-no-kamai.*

Uchidachi senses that shidachi's right wrist is open. He slides his front (right) foot forward and strikes down with his katana. Shidachi quickly pivots his jo clockwise, striking the side of uchidachi's katana (Figure 358). Shidachi will have a left chudan-no-kamai, with the end of his jo pointing at uchidachi's throat. [*Note:* When striking the katana, be sure not to let your jo go past the center of uchidachi's body. Keep a firm grip on the jo and look into uchidachi's eyes at all times.]

In Figure 359, shidachi now slides a half step forward, sliding the jo under uchidachi's right forearm and between his hands, coming to a high left gedan-no-kamai.

Quickly stepping with his right rear foot to the right at a 45-degree angle (migi-maesumi-no-kuzushi), shidachi rotates uchidachi's wrist clockwise and upward (Figure 360).

Shidachi in Figure 361 continues to slide forward with his right foot and pushes clockwise with his jo until the sword comes out of uchidachi's hands.

[*Note:* In practicing this waza, be careful not to apply too much pressure on uchidachi's wrist or you might cause severe injury.]

KATA 6: Chudan Suriage Sumi Migi Ni Kote Guruma Yoko Men

This last technique is very difficult to describe verbally. Here, again, a good teacher is a tremendous asset.

Uchidachi and shidachi start in the proper kamai and in chudan-no-kamai. No more than the first three or four inches of each weapon should be crossing each other as in Figure 362.

The tip of each weapon is dropped to the gedan-no-kamai, and both participants take their required five steps to the rear. After completing this motion, each participant takes the chudan-no-kamai. Uchidachi makes the first motion by sliding his right foot one full step forward, followed immediately by his left foot. Also, simultaneously he raises the boken to jodan-no-kamai (Figure 363). Also simultaneously, shidachi follows the motion, but on his left foot first, followed with the right foot. Shidachi holds chudan-no-kamai.

In Figure 364, Uchidachi steps forward with his rear (right) foot and cuts shidachi's shomen. Simultaneously, shidachi takes a small step to his right with his right foot twisting his body about 20 degrees to his left. As he does so, he rotates his wrist clockwise in a tight, small circle and brings the jo with a snapping motion to the side of the attacking boken.

Once this movement is accomplished, it is imperative that the participants keep the proper distance. Shidachi slides his jo quickly down the side of the boken, where it comes to rest between uchidachi's hands (Figure 365). Shidachi may have to advance both feet slightly to accomplish this movement. The jo's end must remain pointed at uchidachi's throat.

In Figures 366 and 367, Shidachi applies pressure down on uchidachi's left wrist while stepping forward six to eight inches with his right foot, followed by his left foot. Shidachi then brings the end of his jo around and under uchidachi's right forearm until

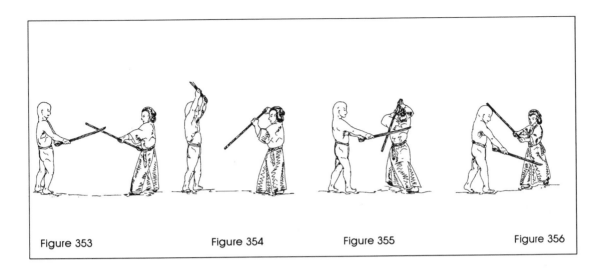

Figure 353   Figure 354   Figure 355   Figure 356

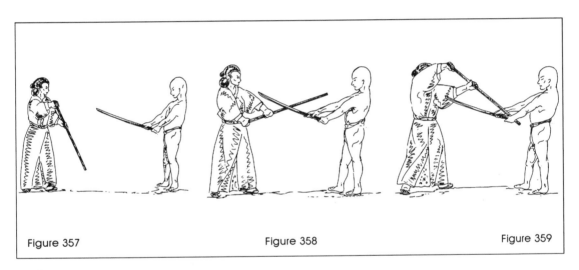

Figure 357   Figure 358   Figure 359

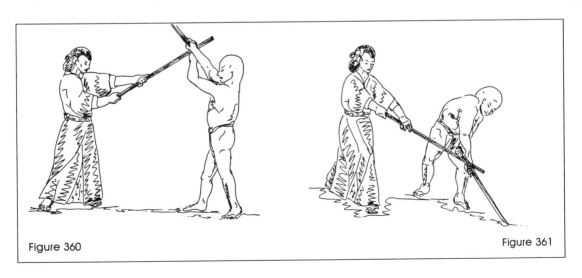

Figure 360   Figure 361

the jo has traveled from six to twelve o'clock and is pointing directly at uchidachi's throat. Keeping pressure against uchidachi's wrist and downward, shidachi takes a step with his left rear foot into migi-maesumi-no-kuzushi. Simultaneously, he makes a popping motion with his left hand. This will force uchidachi to lose his balance, twist his body to the left, and release his hold on the boken.

The waza concludes in Figure 368 with a quick jodan-no-kamai, bringing the jo down on uchidachi's right temple.

* * *

I hope you enjoyed doing the kata as much as we enjoyed presenting it to you. Realize that you cannot comprehend real kata merely by reading this text and mimicking these drawings. You can achieve real understanding only through the eyes and knowledge of a true sensei. Always remember that it is not the kata that makes the performers, but the performer who marvels his audience with his kata. Master Chiba always claimed, "It's not the waza that you must keep a keen eye on, but the technician who has perfected it."

As all things have a beginning, so must they have an ending and, as we say in Texas, we have come to the end of this trail—or, in Japanese, this *do.*

Do. Now here is a good Japanese word. As we have said many times in this book, it means "lane, path, road," and I guess, down in Texas, "a trail." Not just a path or a road that is traveled to go to a specific destination, but one that is traveled a whole life through, seeking perfection in one's quest in life.

The Beginning

NOTES

1. Keiko Fukuda, *Born for the Mat: A Kodokan Kata Textbook for Women Judo,* 5th edition, (Self-published, copyright 1973, Keiko Fukuda, printed in Japan 1973).

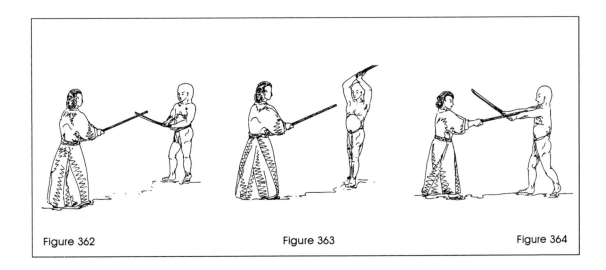

Figure 362

Figure 363

Figure 364

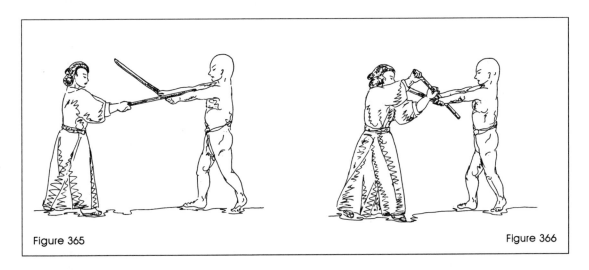

Figure 365

Figure 366

Figure 367

Figure 368

GLOSSARY

AGE   rising
AITA   opponent, adversary
ANZA   sitting cross-legged
ASHI   foot
ASHI-ATE   art of attacking vital spots with the foot
ASHI WAZA   foot and leg techniques
ATEMI WAZA or ATE WAZA   art of attacking vital spots in the body
AWASE WAZA   combination throws
AYUMI-ASHI   ordinary step
BU   military (martial) affairs
BUDO   martial ways
BUJUTSU   martial arts
BUTSUKARI   method of practicing throws up to the point of breaking opponent's
      balance without actually throwing him
CHIKARA   strength
CHUDAN   middle posture with jo
CHUGAERI   forward somersault used in breakfall
DAN   grade or degree indicated by wearing of black belt:
      Shodan—1st Dan
      Nidan—2nd Dan
      Sandan—3rd Dan
      Yodan—4th Dan
      Godan—5th Dan
      Rokudan—6th Dan
      Shichidan—7th Dan
      Hachidan—8th Dan
      Kudan—9th Dan
      Judan—10th Dan

In 1955 Dr. Jigaro Kano's Kodokan still included in his ranking system the ranks of Juichidan and Junidan, more commonly known as the 11th and 12th degree black belt. These ranks were created by Master Kano after he obtained the rank of Judan. At this ceremony he immediately included the higher degrees, stating something similar to, "If you promote me to these degrees, I will immediately add the 13th and 14th degrees. There never can be an end to learning. When reaching the top of one mountain you always find there is another one to climb." It is interesting to note that Master Kano was never promoted above the rank of Judan. After his death in 1938 and before 1955, the Kodokan omitted the 11th and 12th ranks of judo. In my research, I have been unable to find any martial art, in or out of Japan, that includes these higher ranks at the present time. Master Kano is usually credited with creating the ranking system in budo that we know today.

DEBANA   to attack on movement

DO   the trunk of the body

DO   Japanese idiogram *Do,* meaning the path, lane, road, or way in which one travels without veering

DOJO   exercise hall or hall of the way (Do)

ERI   neck band or lapel

EMPI   elbow

FUDOSHIN   imperturbability of mind in an emergency

FUKUSHIKI-KOKYU   deep abdominal breathing

FUMI-KOMI   stepping in

FUSEGI   defense

GAESHI   lock, outer wrist lock

GAESHI WAZA   counter technique or reflex deflection

GARAMI   bent

GENKI   vigor, energy, vitality

GEDAN   lower posture with the jo or hands

GONOSEN-NO-KATA   prearranged demonstration of throws and counter-throws

GYAKU   reverse, adverse; applied to method of choking and holding, *e.g., gyaku juji jime*—reverse necklock or chokelock

HADAKA   naked, *e.g., hadaka jime*—naked chokelock

HANTEI   decision

HAPKIDO   Korean art similar to jujitsu. In Korean, *hap* means to "join" or "coordination"; *ki* denotes the essence of "energy or power"; and *do* means "definition of the art, method or way." Collectively, hapkido therefore means the technique of unarmed combat for self-defense involving skilled application of punches, kicks, blocks, and dodges and the throwing of the opponent using the hands or feet. Hapkido is basically a defensive art.

HOPPO-NO-KUZUSHI   8 directions of off-balance:

(1) *front kuzushi* (mamea-no-kuzushi)

(2) *back kuzushi* (maushiro-no-kuzushi)

(3) *left kuzushi* (hidari-mayoko-no-kuzushi)

(4) *right kuzushi* (migi-mayoko-no-kuzushi)

(5) *right-front-corner kuzushi* (migi-maesumi-no-kuzushi)

(6) *left-front-corner kuzushi* (hidari-maesumi-no-kuzushi)

(7) *right-back-corner kuzushi* (migi-ushirosumi-no-kuzushi)

(8) *Left-back-corner kuzushi* (hidari-ushirosumi-no-kuzushi)

HARA   stomach, abdomen, *e.g., shitahara*—lower abdomen

HARAI   sweep

HASAMI   scissors

HEN-O   adaptation of the situation

HIDARI   left

HIDARI-SHIZENTAI   left natural posture

HIJI   elbow, *e.g., hiji-ate*—attacking vital spots with the elbow

HIKIWAKI   drawn match

HISHIGI   crush, break, lock, as in forearm

HIZA   knee, *e.g., hiza guruma*—knee wheel

HIZA-GASHIRA ATE   attacking vital spots with the kneecap

IPPON   one point (e.g., for a throw) in a contest

JIGOTAI   self-defensive posture

JO   four foot stick, one or one and one-quarter inches thick

JODAN   high posture with the jo or hands

JOZU NA   skillful, adroit (the *o* is a long vowel)

JUDOGI   judo costume

JUDOKA   person practicing judo

JUTSU (JITSU)   art, *e.g., jujutsu*—soft art (*Note: Jujitsu* can also be spelled *jiujitsu,
    jujutsu,* and numerous other ways, but basically all refer to the same art.)

JUJI   cross, *e.g., nami juji jime*—normal cross chokelock

JUKUREN   skill, dexterity, etc.

JU-NO-KATA   slow-motion demonstration of basic principles

KAKE   act of throwing, attack

KAMAI   basic attack and defense posture

KANGEIKO   midwinter judo practice

KANSETSU WAZA   art of bending and twisting the joints

KAPPO   system of resuscitation

KATA   shoulder

KATA   formal system of prearranged exercises in attack and defense. When written with
    another character, the word means "shoulder," *e.g., kata guruma*—shoulder
    wheel. (*Note*: In modern Kodokan judo, there are numerous formal katas
    practiced. The Nage-no-Kata is a required kata for black belt ranks. Still included
    in the Kodokan system is Kodokan Goshin Jutsu Kata. It is not a requirement for
    rank but definitely divides sport judo from self-defense jujutsu.)

KATAME-NO-KATA   prearranged forms of groundwork comprised of holddowns or
    immobilization methods, necklocks, and methods of bending and twisting the
    joints. This kata is made up of 15 techniques.

KATAME WAZA   technique of clinching or immobilization; groundwork

KATSU   system of resuscitation

KEIKO   practice, as opposed to contest

KEITO   to use the wrist for striking (sometimes called chickenhead wrist)

KEIKOGI   practice costume

KESA   scarf, *e.g., kesa gatame* scarf hold, one of the methods of immobilization in
    groundwork

KIAI   (pronounced "Kee-eye") shout supposed to emanate from the lower abdomen
    (*saika tanden* or *shitahara*)

KIBA   straddle, *e.g., kiba-dachi*—straddle stance

KIME-NO-KATA   prearranged methods or forms of defense and attack

KO   small, minor, *e.g., kosoto gari*—minor exterior reap

KOBUSHI-ATE attacking vital spots with the fist

KODOKAN judo headquarters in Tokyo

KOGAN scrotum or testicle

KORYU old style

KOSHI WAZA loin or waist technique

KOTE wrist

KUBI neck, *e.g., kubi gatame*—necklock

KUMI grapple with

KUMI-KATA methods of taking hold of opponent's lapel or belt

KUZURE modified, as in hold or throw

KUZURE break down, *e.g., kuzure kami shiho gatame*—broken upper four quarters

KUZUSHI off balance

KWAI or KAI society, club

KWANSETSU or KANSETSU joint, *e.g., kansetsu waza*—art of bending and twisting the joints

KYU class, grade, rank below black belt (*mudansha*), e.g.:
>   *rokkyu*—6th class
>   *gokyu*—5th class
>   *yokyu*—4th class
>   *sankyu*—3rd class
>   *nikyu*—2nd class
>   *ikkyu*—1st class

KYUSHO vital spot in the body

MA an emphatic prefix, *e.g., masutemi-waza*—throwing in direct lying position

MA-AI proper distance between two partners

MAE-GERI-KEAGE front snap kick

MAITTA exclamation, "I'm beaten!"

MAKI-KOMI roll in, *e.g., soto makikomi*—outer winding throw

MATA thigh, *e.g., uchimata*—inner thigh throw

MAWAI see MA-AI

MIGI right

MIGI SHIZENTAI right natural posture

MITCHAKU SURU to establish contact

MOCHI hold with the hands

MOKUSO or MOKKO meditation, contemplation, reverie

MONTEI disciple or pupil

MOROTE both hands, *e.g., morote seoi nage*—shoulder throw with both hands

MUDANSHA judo pupil below black belt grade. The prefix mu signifies negation—"nothing"

MUNE breast

MURI unreasonable, commonly applied to incorrect use of force when attempting a throw

NAGE throw or to throw

NAGE-NO-KATA prearranged forms of throwing consisting of 15 throws

NESSHIN zeal, enthusiasm, fervor, etc.

NE WAZA groundwork

NIGIRI-KATAMI closing fingers firmly with the thumbs bent underneath, a method supposed to impart resolution and courage to the subject

NYUMON SURU to become a pupil, to join the dojo

O   big, great; the *o* is a long vowel. Hence: *osoto-gari*—major exterior reap

OBI   belt, sash, *e.g., obi otoshi*—belt drop

OCHIRU   pass out due to a strangle hold

OSAE-KOMI WAZA   art of holding, immobilizing the opponent on the ground

OSOTO-GARI   major exterior reap

OSOTO OTOSHI   major outer drop

OUCHIGARI   major internal reap

PISIFORM   small carpal bones

RANDORI   free exercise

REI WO SURU   to perform a salutation

RENZOKU-WAZA   successive technique

RYU   style or school, referring to an old traditional martial art system such as

HOKUSHINKAN CHIBA DOJYO   *Chiba* being the family name; *Hokushin* means north star system; *kan* means hall; and *Dojyo* means way or place. This style or ryu is approximately 750 years old. It was created by the first Chiba fencing master and handed down through 38 generations to its present being.

RYUGI   school, system (the *u* is a long vowel)

SAIKA TANDEN   lower abdomen

SAPPO   attacking vital spots of the body, causing coma or asphyxia

SASAE   support, *e.g., sasae-tsurikomi ashi*—supporting foot lift pull throw

SASOI   inductive

SASOKU   left side

SENSEI   teacher

SEOI   carry on the shoulder, *e.g., seoi nage*—shoulder throw

SEIZA   sitting on knees

SHIAI   contest

SHIBORI   strangle, choke, *e.g., shibori waza*—technique of choking or strangling

SHIDACHI   the defender in kata

SHIHAN   the title *Shihan* ("Doctor" or "Past Master") is conferred on a martial artist who has been promoted in a particular ryu with a teaching certification. This could be compared to a deacon or elder in a church, or someone who is held in high esteem due to his knowledge or financial support of the ryu. This title is indicative of a station and totally indigenous to the ryu. It is an honorary title sometimes translated to mean "Master Teacher," which would be a very loose translation but somewhat correct. It is usually given to someone within the ryu for his total support of the ryu; it does not necessarily mean that he is master of the art. (*Note:* In today's Japan, to receive this title, you must have the rank of godan or above in that ryu. Many people claim this title, but very few have actually received it from a traditional Japanese ryu.)

SHIHO   four directions, *e.g., kami shiho gatame*—locking of upper four quarters.

SHIME   choking

SHIME WAZA   art of choking

SHINTAI   Advance or retreat—foot movement in judo. Written with another character, it also means "body."

SHISEI   posture

SHIZEN HONTAI   fundamental natural posture

SHIZENTAI   natural posture

SHITAHARA   lower abdomen (the *i* is mute, *i.e., shitahara*)

SHOBU   announcing the beginning of a playoff match. Also, the start of a playoff after the players have returned to their center locations

SHOCHUGEIKO   midsummer judo practice

SODE   sleeve, *e.g., sode guruma*—sleeve wheel. The old terminology also means method of choking

SUMI   corner, *e.g., sumi-gaeshi*—corner throw

SUTEMI WAZA   art of throwing in a lying position. The *sutemi* means literally "self-abandonment." It is pronounced "stemi."

TACHI WAZA   art of throwing in a standing position

TAI   body, *e.g., tai-otoshi*—body drop

TAI-SABAKI   turning movement

TANDEN   abdomen

TATAMI   a mat used for covering a Japanese floor. The Kodokan's first dojo, established in 1882, was referred to as a 12-tatami room, which would make the size of the room twelve by eighteen foot. This was a normal way of measuring a room or house in those days. Today's Kodokan boasts over one thousand tatamis.

TE   hand, also trick

TENKAN   to turn over, roll over, etc.

TE WAZA   hand technique

TEKUBI   wrist

TOKUI   favorite throw or technique

TORITE   "taker" (the partner that effects the throw) in kata or prearranged forms

TSUKI   thrust

TSUKIAGE   rising punch

TSUGI ASHI   following foot, method of foot movement in judo

TSUKURI   destroying balance or fitting action for attack (kake). The first *u* is almost mute, i.e., "Tskuri."

TSURIKOMI   lift-pull on opponent's collar and sleeve

TSUYOI   strong, powerful

UCHI   interior, *e.g., uchi mata*—inner thigh throw

UCHIDACHI   the attacker in prearranged practice

UCHI WAZA   striking techniques

UDE   arm, *e.g., ude-garami*—entangled arm lock in kansetsu waza

UDE-ATE   art of attacking vital spots with the arm

UKEMI   method of falling in breakfall; literally, "falling way"

UKETE   "receiver" in kata or prearranged forms of attack and defense

UKE   attacker or one who floats

UKI   to float, *e.g., uki waza*—floating throw

URA   opposite, reverse, obverse, etc., *e.g., ura nage*—rear throw

USHIRO-TEKUBI   holding both hands behind the back

WAZA   trick, skill, technique

YAMA   mountain, *e.g., yama-arashi*—mountain storm throw

YAWARA   the original name of jujitsu. For a period of time both words were used, but always referring to the same art. By the turn of the twentieth century, the word *yawara* was no longer in use. *Jujutsu* was changed to *taiho jutsu* (body techniques used exclusively by military and law enforcement agencies), and Dr. Jigaro Kano's new judo was well established.

YOKO   side, hence: *yoko guruma*—side wheel throw

YUDANSHA   holder of the Dan grade (black belt) in Japanese martial arts

ABOUT THE AUTHOR

DARRELL MAX CRAIG received his initiation into the martial arts in 1956 while assigned to the Third Marine Division in Yokusaka, Japan. He began his martial arts career with the study of karate under Master Gogen Yamaguchi of the Goju School. Mr. Craig was transferred to Okinawa in 1958, where he furthered his study of karate and began a study of Okinawan weapons, a style of weaponry historically unique to that island. In 1970 Mr. Craig began his study of kendo under Sensei Yajima. Later, in 1974, he began his study of taiho jitsu under Sensei Ichiro Hata. In 1973 he received the highest recognition in his career when he was awarded the title of Shihan by the All-Japan Karate-do Federation. Shihan is an historical title of the army of the feudal warlords and has been retained as a term of great respect in modern Japan. The title has been bestowed upon very few westerners.

During his ca   cessfully in many high-level kendo an   se instructor for numerous governme   **Date Due**   ived commenda-tions from the Hou   ious service. Mr. Craig currently oper   ditional Japanese martial arts school at   ught.

Darrell Craig h   ) in each of Shito Ryu karate, Junse Go   Okinawan Shorin kobudo; yodan (4th   do; and sandan (3rd Dan) in osae ail   *awing the Sword,* (Tuttle, 1981).